MW01244390

FROM WHERE SHALL COME OUR HELP?

The Lament of Abused Persons

Henry Onwusoro Ogbuji

En Route Books and Media, LLC
Saint Louis, MO

ENROUTE
Make the time

En Route Books and Media, LLC
5705 Rhodes Avenue
St. Louis, MO 63109

Cover credit: Sebastian Mahfood

ISBN-13: 979-8-88870-021-1
Library of Congress Control Number: 2022951969

DEDICATION

For Rebecca Oruma and all abused persons

LIST OF ABBREVIATIONS

CAN   Christian Association of Nigeria

FIDA   Federacion Internacionale De Abogadas

JDPC   Justice, Development and Peace Commission

MCEE   Ministry of Compassion, Emancipation and Empowerment

WSG   Women Support Group

TABLE OF CONTENTS

Section I: The Dynamics of Domestic Violence in Nigeria

Section II: Vision

ACKNOWLEDGEMENTS

Granted a work of this nature and magnitude requires solitude, yet it cannot be accomplished without the support of others. As I shared thoughts with those around me about this publication, I received amazing responses from them; they all assured me that the title is topical, and some went the length of providing me with helpful insights and/or resources. These include Fr. Ignatius Nze, Fr. Maxwell Berechi, and Fr. Richard Santerre and Kathy Kelleher both of Youville House Cambridge, Massachusetts. MaryAnn Harold, owner of 89.3 FM radio station Boston, leader of the Adoration Team and Legion of Mary was a solid spur to this publication. I am eternally grateful to you all for your support and encouragement.

I am profoundly grateful to those who had time to go through my manuscript, made useful insights, and inscribed a note on this book. They are Nicolette Manglos-Weber, who wrote the Foreword, and Luis Menendez-Antuna and Aloy Sunny Ochasi, who inscribed the notes at the back cover page of the book. I am indebted to Most Rev. Anthony J.V Obinna (Emeritus Archbishop of Owerri) for providing me the opportunity for further studies after my ordination, and to my local ordinary, Most Rev. Lucius Ugorji and his auxiliary bishop Most Rev. Moses Chikwe. I appreciate the fraternal solidarity of the brother priests who lived with me at St. Joseph's rectory, Boston, during my research and writing, namely Fr. Alex Okere, Fr. Malachy Obiejesi, Fr. Patrick Alemayo, Fr. Henry Nwanguma, Fr. Modestus Nwanna and Fr. Gustav Miracle. The hospitality of the pastor, Fr. Brian McHaugh, and the decorum of the rectory provided me the serenity and space for my research and writing.

To my mom, Nneoma Grace Ogbuji, my siblings, Agatha, James and Matilda and their spouses, Callistus, Monica and David, I say 'thanks' for your huge support and understanding. I appreciate the support of my friends, Fr. Maxwell, Dr. Charles, Rosemary and Gina throughout the writing of this thesis. The prayers and good wishes of my friend and mentor, Fr. Andrew Nkwocha, cannot be easily forgotten. Finally, I thank everyone who shared thoughts with me and provided me any materials that helped me in the course of my writing this piece. My profound gratitude goes to you all.

FOREWORD

For decades, domestic violence has been the purview of global health experts, development policymakers, and feminist social scientists. These fields have established the personal and collective harm that ripples out from domestic violence, and they have made human rights-based arguments for sanctioning such violence in its diverse forms across cultures. Yet theological treatments of the issue have been rare, and they have even less often addressed domestic violence in settings like West Africa, where colonial injustices and uneven inculturation processes challenge the work of intercultural theological ethics.

Why is a contextualized, practical theological intervention into this issue necessary? For at least two reasons. The first is a pragmatic one: West Africans are by most measures very religious people, for whom theological arguments—Christian or Muslim, as the case may be—hold significant weight for social and relational ethics. Particularly in Nigeria, religious leaders, texts, and ideas have a unique authority, extending into the most intimate settings of the home and the most public sites of national politics. If theological leaders neglect the issue, then its neglect will continue to be normalized.

The second reason is more philosophical, but no less important. Among global health experts and policymakers, debates about domestic violence often get caught in a stalemate between two frameworks: the universalizing ideals of Western liberalism vs. a critical cultural relativism. Neither perspective is up to the task of dismantling domestic violence. The former sweeps all cultural differences up in its path, minimizing histories and domestic institutions, and promoting cookie cutter solutions from Lagos to Mumbai. The relativist position, on the other hand, too often resigns itself to pervasive social harm to avoid the stain of cultural imperialism.

In the current work, *From Where Will Come Our Help?*, Henry Ogbuji sets out an alternative rationale and framework for addressing domestic violence, based in Christian theological ethics and targeted at the global Catholic Church. Ogbuji communicates the need to address the issue at two separate levels: via the political advocacy of church leaders and in settings of pastoral care. By grounding his approach in Christian teaching on the dignity of the person without regard to gender and the non-dualism of body and spirit, Ogbuji makes a theological case for transforming a systemic cultural reality.

Ogbuji also brings that theological case into dialogue with social theory and history. As a work of practical theology, the book is interdisciplinary and integrative. In the first section, the book lays out the problem, both internationally and in Nigeria, sensitively diagnosing a cultural ill with reference to Christian and indigenous patriarchy, colonial oppression, and the collective trauma of civil war. In the second section, the book engages theological and sociological resources on human dignity, social power, and inculturation, and begins to outline some policy solutions involving church-state cooperation. In the third section, the book applies the principle of compassion for the suffering to the pastoral tasks of preaching and counseling, and it presents strategies for institutionalizing a compassionate response within seminary instruction.

One of the book's major strengths is its attention to the spiritual abuse that befalls women in relation to their religious traditions. Few social scientists have the conceptual resources to explore this aspect of the domestic abuse experience, as important as it is, and Ogbuji's work does much to fill in that gap. The concept of spiritual abuse is newly emergent in the literature and demands more robust and contextualized analyses, and Ogbuji's work rises to this occasion. Indeed, I was eager to read more on this topic once I'd finished the current volume, and I greatly hope more scholars will pursue nuanced investigations of spiritual abuse in postcolonial contexts and connect them to the broader conversation, which so far has focused on the religiously deconstructing North Atlantic.

Similarly, Ogbuji's discussion of theological anthropology deftly treats the dangers of Christian Platonic dualism on the one hand, and empiricist materialism on the other. These polar philosophical traditions both falter in their treatment of domestic abuse, by failing to understand the unity of soul and body, and the theological import of violence against bodies in turn. One can see how, even today, theological writers reveal their dualist assumptions by neglecting to address this issue at all; public health and sociological writers reveal their materialism by neglecting its spiritual and theological dimensions. Ogbuji makes an exceptionally strong case that these facets of the human—and domestic violence is a human experience—must be observed and cared for in tandem. This is where Ogbuji reveals not just a rationale for a theological treatment of domestic violence, but also the virtues of theologizing outside of the American and Eurocentric canon.

As I concluded my reading of the book, I wondered about how Nigerian women themselves imagine and enact social power regarding domestic violence, and about women-led strategies for addressing the problem and caring for victims, whether within the church or without. As Ogbuji writes, in his ministerial work he has heard these women speak time and time again. I hope in future works we readers will hear from these women, too—so the complexities of their heartbreak *and* agency, wounds *and* healing rituals would come through.

Similarly, I wondered about the historical figures and current-day activists Ogbuji names in the final passages of the book's first section, and their shared theological imagination. For the women who stormed the floor of the National Assembly after the failure of the Gender Equality Bill, what role does Christian theology play in how they understand their activism? This would be a fruitful next inquiry following Ogbuji's work of lament: what types of theologies, ethics, and communities are born from the lament of women suffering violence, to use the language of theologian Emmanuel Katongole?[1]

Asserting the dignity of all persons as a theological principle is easy to do; revering that dignity in practice is much harder. It is especially difficult given the legacies of dehumanization those living today inherit, within and outside of the church. Misogyny and anti-

---

[1] Emmanuel Katongole, *Born from Lament: The Theology and Politics of Hope in Africa.* Eerdmans, 2017.

Blackness are two of most pervasive and relevant to the current issue. Like Ogbuji, my own work is indebted to Mercy Oduyoye; often when I write I hear her cautionary words about the dangers of Euro-American women and African men studying the experience of African women without true solidarity or identification.[2]

I read Ogbuji's work as an important effort toward such identification, and one that should open rather than end the conversation. I eagerly anticipate the implementation of Ogbuji's proposed strategies within the Nigerian Catholic organization and how they might connect and collaborate with existing women-led activism. And I look for the institutionalization of healing for abused persons within the church, both in Nigeria and elsewhere, to rebuild a Christian ethical community for the dignity of all persons.

Nicolette D. Manglos-Weber
Assistant Professor of Religion and Society
School of Theology
Boston University
Boston, MA

---

[2] Mercy Oduyoye, *Daughters of Anowa: African Women and Patriarchy*. Orbis Books, 1995, p. 82.

PREFACE

There was a professor of mine during my doctoral studies who was good at bringing guest professors to spice up the learning experience, an exercise that helped broaden my intellectual horizon. On one occasion, he brought in a professor of Nigerian origin, a professor of Political Science, to lecture on "Religion, Gender and Sexuality" from a Nigerian context. She spoke about the marginalization of women in Nigeria, and how the patriarchal structure of the Nigerian society leaves women at the margins of governance. She was a smart academician and a woman of eloquence with an admirable power of articulation. Her presentation impressed many of us, and some students asked intelligent questions to which she did justice, so to speak. My question came last as I waited to find out if any of my fellow students could observe what I perceived as a lacuna in her lecture (a few of my cohort were fellow Nigerians).

Born and bred in Nigeria – though now a professor in the US – and dealing with such subject matter as Religion, Gender and Sexuality, I expected our guest professor to highlight how cultural and religious elements impact life and activities of Nigerian women. One would suppose that a mention would be made of domestic violence or violence against women as a challenge to the participation of the Nigerian woman in the public space. (By now, I have started thinking about this publication). How can we discuss Gender and Sexuality in the Nigerian socio-political context without any mention of domestic violence and violence against women? The professor's response to my question about the place of domestic violence appeared more intriguing than her not making it a part of the discourse. Her answer was to the effect that domestic violence is not a problem and, if it is, it is a global issue. "Even here in the US, there are cases of domestic violence," she said in part in her reply. What she said we cannot totally dismiss. Domestic violence and violence against women is not a phenomenon particular to Nigeria; it is as she said a global matter. The troubling question is: Does the fact that it is a pandemic make it less a problem in the development and empowerment of the Nigerian women and children?

What makes domestic violence in Nigeria a worrisome matter is its prevalence. The frequency, forms and responses to the phenomenon help us to understand the magnitude of the problem in a given society. Largely, the responses of leadership (civil as well as ecclesial) determine the frequency and, sometimes, the form of abuse. Societies that criminalize domestic violence dynamize its mitigation. Where there are institutions and structures that support victims and survivors of abuse, victims and survivors cope better with the situation, overwhelming as it is. In Nigeria, as in most African nations, the laws do not criminalize domestic violence; legislation is conspicuously androcentric. The culture and structures of Nigerian society and her institutions have normalized it. Thus, as far as the Nigerian socio-cultural context is concerned, familial violence is not a problem. Little wonder the prevalence of the phenomenon in Nigeria. Only when you consider something a problem do you start excogitating possible solutions. I think that it is this internalizing and normalizing scenario that impacted our Nigerian professor in a foreign land.

Come to think about it: the emotional and physical abuse that children witness or suffer in the hands of parents, elder siblings, extended family members, teachers, and the bullying from schoolmates and authorities; the sexual, emotional and physical abuses that husbands, family, boyfriends, bosses subject women to. Arguably, we all witness or experience domestic violence at various stages and times in life. In my dozen years of ministry in Nigeria, matters of domestic violence were one of the frequently recurring pastoral issues that I encountered and engaged with. The impunity of the menfolk to abuse women and children was very provocative. The experience made me to reminisce constantly the violence I witnessed as a child growing up in an extended family setting.

The decision to embark on this publication was born out of the desire to confront the oddity of the dominant Nigerian culture and worldview and to present an alternative narrative and worldview at the table. It is an invitation to greater and profound theological and scholarly discourse on this subject matter and the myriads of violence and dehumanizing phenomena that our most vulnerable population in Nigeria and Africa suffer. The title of the book *From Where Shall Come Our Help?* comes from the lament of the Psalmist (Ps 121:1) who hopes for divine guidance and protection. I imagine abused persons who have lost hope in church and society cry and lament like the Psalmist for divine intervention. They are crushed in a system they meaningfully belong to, but that sadly treats them unfairly.

The human person is the subject matter of many disciplines including theology. The pain and suffering that humans experience belong to the field of pastoral and practical theology. While much research and theological discussions have been dedicated to domestic violence in the western academic world, it is scarcely a matter of interest in Africa. It is my hope that this publication will serve as "an episodic event" that would trigger responses and discussions about the gender-based injustice meted to people for no fault of theirs especially as it affects the Church. I must recognize the great of work of Mercy Oduyoye, who in her book *Daughters of Anowa: African Women and Patriachy* highlighted and bemoaned the Church's role in perpetuating the subjugation of women in Nigeria and in the African continent. The expectation is to provide hope to abused persons, challenge civil and ecclesial leadership as well as offer a handy material for theological studies and debate.

INTRODUCTION

For the third time (2021), the Gender Equality Bill is on the floor of Nigeria's National Assembly and it is very uncertain it would see the light of the day. The bill, sponsored by one of the few female senators, faced many criticisms by the male-dominated legislature at its first reading such that raises doubt if it would pass second reading on the floor of the upper house of the ninth Assembly. Fundamentally, the Gender Equality Bill seeks to eliminate all forms of discrimination against women and guarantees equal opportunity, development and advancement of all citizens of Nigeria irrespective of their gender. The provisions of the bill include, the instruction that all government, public and private institutions take adequate measures to provide equal remuneration of persons of equal skill, competence, enterprise and knowledge; the prohibition of sexual and domestic violence against women, and the rights of widows who are subjected to inhuman treatments; consolidation of government and community protection of all citizens, and the promotion of peace and harmony in homes where members are guaranteed equal access and treatment against discrimination.[3]

Unfortunately, but typical of Nigerian society, the bill suffered massive attacks on religious grounds among others. A Muslim legislator vehemently opposed the bill beginning from its title saying

---

[3] Linda Akibi, "Gender Equality Bill Suffers Setback in the Senate," Channels TV (Nigeria), December 18, 2021, www.channelstv.com.

that the language of "equality" of men and women offends the sensibilities of Islamic faith. He argues that equality of man and woman infringes on the practice of Islamic religion. The sponsor of the bill tried to make some concessions but it was not enough to take the bill to second reading. The bill sponsor was ready to have further consultations with those opposed to the bill.[4] We recall that a similar bill, Gender Equality Opportunities Bill (GEOB) in 2016 suffered same fate with a Christian lawmaker joining his Muslim counterparts to declare the bill unacceptable because it contradicts his Christian religious belief.[5] Therefore, for the third time (the bill was first introduced to the National Assembly in 2010 also by a woman legislator), the Gender Equality Bill is going to be quashed principally for religious reasons. A crucial question arises about where the lawmakers draw the line between religion and lawmaking.

Following the persistent reluctance of the lawmakers to pass women related bills,[6] some Nigerian women stormed the National Assembly to register their dismay. In the report of the protest as told by the Punch newspaper of March 2, 2022, the women expressed their disappointment over the reluctance of the legislative house to address issues of women despite the assurances of the legislature. As

---

[4] Akibi, "Gender Equality Bill Suffers Setback in the Senate."

[5] Damilola Agbalajobi and Leke Oluwalogbon, "The Nigerian Senate and the Politics of the Non-passage of the Gender Equality Bill," *African Journal of Political Science and International Relations* 13, no. 3 (April 2019): 22.

[6] There are, indeed, several bills about the well-being and rights of women before the National Assembly.

characteristic of the Nigerian government, the gate of the house chambers was shut against the protesters who tried to register that gender equality is not simply about women's welfare but about the development of the country.[7]

The reality is that the highly patriarchal nature of the Nigerian society and the rigid adherence to religious beliefs and practices constitute a worrisome threat to the dignity and rights of women, and effectuate the perpetuation of domestic violence in the Nigerian polity. This cuts across the institutions and agents of socialization namely, family, schools, peer groups, and religious congregations. Faith communities' recourse to their doctrines and Holy Books to perpetrate violence against women reinforce the culturally patriarchal structure. To be a woman in Nigeria becomes synonymous with victim of abuse. Such scenario leaves victims of domestic violence more or less in perpetual suffering and pain, and with no claims to their inalienable human dignity and rights.

Statistically, this work proves that domestic violence is prevalent in the Nigerian society. It provides evidence that the West African Country has the history of disrespect for the dignity and rights of women and children who constitute largely the victims of familial violence. The book implicates the church, the culture and the government for the gross oppression and marginalization of the vulnerable population of their communities and country. How may a leader transcend their cultural, religious, ethnic, social, and political

[7] Solomon Odeniyi, "Women Protest at National Assembly over Rejected Bills," *The Punch Newspaper* (Nigeria), March 2, 2022.

identities, and excel in the responsibility of engendering transformational leadership when confronted with such challenge as violence against women and children? How could leadership function to bring about a safe and flourishing environment for everyone, irrespective of age and gender, to thrive? How may the Nigerian Church respond pastorally to the prevalent cases of domestic violence among their members and in their communities in such a way that brings them healing and human flourishing? How can the Nigerian civil and ecclesial leadership create a safe environment for her most vulnerable citizens? Here, we are set to engage the above questions in order to bring to the awareness of the Church her duty to minister to the needs of her most needy members. It challenges church leaders and communities to provide prompt, adequate and compassionate pastoral responses and resources to abused persons and to stand to condemn it, evil as it is.

There are not many researches on the subject matter of domestic violence in Nigeria. The bunch of researches on the phenomenon come from the social sciences and reproductive health. There is rarely any theological literature on the subject matter in the West African nation. This publication is an effort to loan a theological voice to this structure of sin that has eaten deep into the Nigerian socio-cultural and religious fabric. It argues that the Church (and other faith bodies) as a moral authority has so much to do in the elimination of domestic violence in the Nigerian space. It considers domestic violence as an ecclesial matter that requires religious and pastoral leadership response. With the evidence of the results of researches on the role of spirituality and proper pastoral response to victims and survivors of sexual and domestic violence,[8] we submit that appropriate and prompt response of faith communities and religious leadership fosters the healing, emancipation and empowerment of abused persons in society. It is our expectation that the Nigerian Church will achieve this missionary work through a compassionate ministry that is participatory and praxis-oriented.

For the purpose of an ordered articulation, we have divided this work into three sections. Section I, which consists of five chapters, considers the dynamics of the phenomenon of domestic violence in the Nigeria society. It defines, provides a panoramic history of domestic violence and gives and overview of the book (chapter 1). It exposes the socio-cultural beliefs and practices that perpetuate abuse (chapter2), enumerates the forms and highlights the alarming consequences of familial violence on victims, community and society (chapter 3). By detailing the insensibility of the government to the plight of women and her reluctance to enact women empowering laws, it expounds how the Nigerian state is complicit with marital violence (chapter 4). The section concludes by discussing the failure of the Nigerian Church in her religious and moral duty to respond adequately to this phenomenon and raises critical questions meant to challenge ecclesial leadership to reassess her pastoral ministerial

---

[8] James Kennedy, Robert Davis, and Bruce Taylor, "Changes in Spirituality and Well-Being among Victims of Assault," *Journal for the Scientific Study of Religion* 37, no. 2 (June 1998); and Dawnovise N. Fowler and Michele A. Rountree, "Exploring the Meaning and Role of Spirituality for Women Survivors of Intimate Partner Abuse," *The Journal of Pastoral Care and Counseling* 63, no. 3 (September 2009).

assumptions and suppositions (chapter 5). The section contends that in a context where the socio-cultural factors perpetuate violence and there are no resources for abused persons, the Church can be a strong support system to them. This leads us to a discussion on our vision for the Nigerian Church and society in the next section.

In Section II, we share our vision for the victims of domestic violence, family, church and the Nigerian society. The section focuses on the defense of the dignity and rights of victims of familial violence in Nigeria and its implications for ecclesial and civil leadership. It makes submission to respect and dignity of abused persons by presenting a theological anthropology that affirms the spark of the divine in all humans irrespective of gender and societal status (chapter 6). It considers the image of the church as an evangelizing and empowering community for the Nigerian culture (chapter 7). The final chapter of the section (chapter 8) discusses the concept of power especially in scriptural and ecclesial contexts, and the necessity of holding violence perpetrators accountable. The chapter argues that a collaboration of ecclesial and civil authorities is crucial for a healthy and just Nigerian society. This leads us to the next section, which deals with a theological-pastoral model required for concrete action.

Section III - Social Transformation - considers concrete pastoral approaches and steps toward the desired transformation. It develops the theological concept of compassion as a concrete action of identification with the violated, and discusses God as a compassionate Father (chapter 9). The Life and Ministry of Jesus provides us an exemplar of a compassionate God and challenges us to be as compassionate and to show solidarity with the violated of our communities and the world (chapter 10). Concrete compassionate praxis-oriented response by the church to mitigate domestic violence includes a broadening and restructure of the seminary and parish curricula (chapter 11), compassion-praxis preaching (chapter 12), and pastoral counseling and support for victims (chapter 13). Ultimately, we submit that adequate pastoral response to domestic violence is a risky venture but worth the risk.

SECTION I

THE DYNAMICS
OF DOMESTIC VIOLENCE IN NIGERIA

CHAPTER ONE

MEANING, HISTORY AND OVERVIEW
OF DOMESTIC VIOLENCE

What Are We Talking About?

Abuse involves the violation of the dignity and rights person(s). It is a violent or cruel action towards others that results in harming or injuring them. While there are various kinds of abuse, our focus here is domestic violence or abuse. Domestic violence refers to a pattern of abusive behaviors by one or both parties who are in an intimate relationship such as marriage, family, friendship, dating or cohabitation. World Health Organization (WHO) defines domestic violence as the use of physical force, threatened or actual, against oneself, someone else, a group of persons or community, which causes or has the likelihood of causing injury, mental harm, maldevelopment, deprivation or death.[9] Because it mostly occurs in the context of the home or intimate relationship, it is often referred to as intimate partner violence, marital violence or familial violence. Domestic violence is an intentional and persistent act of violation against another (usually in the home) in a way that causes pain, distress or injury. It is an abusive treatment of one family member by another,

---

[9] Awawu Grace Nmadu et al., "Cross-sectional Study on Knowledge, Attitude and Prevalence of Domestic Violence among Women in Kaduna, North-west Nigeria," *BMJ Open* (March 2022): 1.

which violates their fundamental human rights and integrity. Domestic violence includes battering of intimate partners and others, sexual abuse of children, marital rape, and traditional practices that are harmful to women.[10]

Domestic violence, accordingly, is not a single act but a pattern of behavior that is abusive, has the intent to showcase power and exercise control over another. In the end, someone is deprived of his or her rights and their dignity trampled upon. Throughout this piece, we use domestic violence, familial violence, marital violence, intimate partner violence, violence against women and child abuse interchangeably.

Mostly, domestic violence is divided into partner abuse and child abuse. We shall consider both kinds of abuse. In the Nigerian context, women are mostly the victims of familial violence and so constitute the primary focus of this book. This is by no means suggesting that only women constitute victims of domestic violence. Women also abuse men, as we shall see in the next chapter. However, the dominant narrative presents a scenario of gender-based violence. Hence, we shall use domestic violence and violence against women interchangeably. This opens up the understanding of violence or violence against women as "the annihilation of connectivity, the dulling and erasure of human relationality through objectification."[11] Therefore, in talking about abuse of persons, we are

---

[10] Ose N. Aihie, "Prevalence of Domestic Violence in Nigeria: Implications for Counselling," *Edo Journal of Counselling* 2, no. 1 (May 2009): 1.

[11] Pamela Cooper-White, *The Cry of Tamar: Violence against Women and the Church's Response*, 2nd ed. (Minneapolis: Fortress Press, 2012), 41.

speaking of the understanding and role of power in human (intimate) relationships where one sees or relates to the other more as an object than as a subject.

When we talk about the Church, we refer primarily to the Catholic Church. The author is a Catholic priest and believes that the popularity, influence and structure of the Catholic Church in Nigeria as in most countries of the world accords her a privileged place to play a significant role in society. We all (Clergy, Religious and Lay) are the Church; however, the word "Church" here is often used to refer to ecclesial leadership to challenge their attitude to the phenomenon. Nevertheless, other ecclesial bodies (and indeed other religious bodies including the Muslims) are not left out in the call to support and promote the course of women empowerment and ensure the mitigation of domestic violence. We believe that the religious bodies' commitment to the course of abuse of vulnerable persons would constitute a milestone in addressing the subject matter in both private and public spaces in the country and in the world.

How Did We Get Here?

Domestic Violence is a phenomenon that knows no boundaries of race, color, age, sexual orientation, gender, nationality, religion or culture. It is an expression of persons' attitude to exercise power and control over others. Sexual and domestic violence is a matter, which many people are uncomfortable talking about. In her article, "Familial Violence against Women as a Challenge for Theology and Ethics," Andrea Lehner- Hartmann expresses concern that domestic violence is not a popular topic for political, theological or ethical discussions. She attributes this situation of neglect to a natural and self-protective reaction due to the vicarious traumatization that is associated with violence.[12] It is equally true that most men do not talk about it simply because they believe that male supremacy is non-negotiable.

Recent scholarship has considerable literature on the subject matter of sexual and domestic violence especially from the feminist writers. Feminist scholarship has been able to trace a long history of this domineering and controlling attitude by men in efforts to have women subjugated to their authority. For example, Catherine Kroeger and Nancy Nason-Clark draw our attention to the fact that ancient Greek tradition had it that, women are made of an inferior substance as a cruel trick of the gods to strip men of their potential.[13]

The Judeo-Christian tradition from the account of the woman's creation from the side of the man (Gen 2:21-22) paints a picture of men as naturally higher than women in the order of creation. Pamela Cooper-White, presenting a feminist perspective, explains that Ancient and Judeo-Christian civilizations for about four thousand years understood power as the ability to manage and control others. This worldview, which goes back to the earliest establishment of a culture was monotheistic and patriarchal and thus the prerogative

---

[12] Andrea Lehner-Hartmann, "Familial Violence against Women as a Challenge for Theology and Ethics," in *When 'Love' Strikes: Social Sciences, Ethics and Theology on Family Violence*, ed. Annemie Dillen (Leuven, Belgium: Peeters, 2009), 109.

[13] Catherine Kroeger and Nancy Nason-Clark, *No Place for Abuse*, rev. ed. (Downers Grove, IL: Inter Varsity Press), 118.

of men.[14] Power in this normative sense, as Cooper-White explains, implies power-over or lordship over others. In this sense, the measure of one's power is one's ability to have authority and control over a large number of persons and properties. The Darwinian understanding of power mirrors this worldview in its construct of the world as a place for scrambling, striving, and competition. Life is about a constant struggle that ends up with the survival of the fittest. Going by this mindset, what one gets is a chain of lordship and servitude with everyone either over others or under them. This perpetuates a situation where the powerful protect themselves and those under them against their perceived rivals while at the same time working hard to be at the top of the power ladder. This concept of power, for most feminist scholars, no matter how it is neatly packaged, has a faulty and harmful foundation namely, an anthropology of fear and might, and enmeshed in masculinity.[15]

Dorothea Timmers-Huigens in her article, "Christian Faith and Justification of Domestic violence" insists that Christianity played a key role in the perpetuation of domestic violence through the centuries. She maintains that the Church reproduced the Greco-Roman culture that justified violence against women and children and detailed how Christian literature and teachings legitimized violence in homes.[16] Timmers-Huigens argues that the Christian theology of

---

[14] Cooper-White, *The Cry of Tamar*, 54.

[15] Cooper-White, *The Cry of Tamar*, 54.

[16] Dorothea Timmers-Huigens, "Christian Faith and Justification of Domestic Violence," in *When 'Love' Strikes: Social Sciences, Ethics and Theology on Family Violence*, ed. Annemie Dillen (Leuven, Belgium: Peeters, 2009), 178-186.

suffering which sees every human suffering as redemptive helped to reinforce domestic violence. According to her:

> Time and again the argument remains the same: suffering is justified because it belongs to the common ordering of things; that a human does not deserve any better than to suffer; and that a Christian should love the suffering since it brings him into contact with the suffering of Christ. Suffering is considered to be purification, and therefore one should carry one's cross patiently.[17]

This understanding of suffering, Timmers-Huigens insists, encouraged violence in the homes by the acclaimed heads of the family (men) against women and children; men abused children and women physically and emotionally in the name of discipline and the abused accepted it in obedience as to God in order to attain a heavenly reward.

Western civilization imbibed this culture of abuse for a longtime, continues feminist scholarship. It believes however, that a lot has changed in modern times. Democratization of many post-modern societies is beginning to recognize the dignity and rights of women and children and taking measures to eliminate violence against the most vulnerable. Indeed, considerable changes have taken place in terms of culture, particular kinds of government, and technological advancement over the period. Again, there are varied

---

[17] Timmers-Huigens, "Christian Faith and Justification of Domestic Violence," 176.

cultural variations that exist between and among the various continents and countries of the world. However, many feminists lament the widespread of modern patriarchal systems that still operate with the mentality of power as the "power of lordship or dominion over others" mindset.

This feminist position sounds too general or presumptuous. Cooper-White cautions against the allurement to blend in the various cultural systems of male dominance. She argues that such generalization may not reflect the actual experiences of men and women in different patriarchal cultures but may only be ideological and reductionistic.[18] However, patriarchy prevails in many modern societies and seems resistant to change. Consequently, repeatedly, there are concrete and disgusting cases of domestic violence in a frequency that is not ignorable across the nations of the world. This is especially true in Africa where the cultures are hugely patriarchal. Our study has a focus on Nigeria, a West African nation and the largest country in the continent. Our statistics and study would show that the phenomenon is prevalent in the Nigerian society even as it challenges the church to step up its responsibility to stem the tide. We want to acknowledge that social media have helped to reveal and bring to the public space many awful cases of domestic violence which otherwise would have remained covert.

---

[18] Cooper-White, *The Cry of Tamar*, 54.

What is Going On?

In the fall of 2021, report had it that the Nigerian police, following her husband's instructions, manhandled a woman who sought for divorce from her marriage. Lantana Isiyaku, 25, from north-west of the country, who filed for divorce from her marriage with her husband, Umar Ibrahim, was forced to strip herself naked while two police officers of the defunct Special Anti-Robbery Squad (SARS) brutalized her in the presence of her estranged husband. According to the story, Lantana won the court ruling over battery, neglect and economic abuse by her husband who was also married to two other women. Umar accused the judge of insidious and surreptitious relations with his wife and consequently appealed to a sharia court that now granted judgment to his favor. On the refusal of Lantana to return to Umar's home following the sharia court verdict, the angry Umar contracted police anti-robbery squad to discipline Lantana and coerce her to return to his house. During the assault, the police insisted on knowing the sponsor(s) of her litigation before the court.[19]

The above story gives us a glimpse of the fate of victims of domestic violence in Nigeria. It helps us grasp the agony and helplessness of the Nigerian woman before the male dominated society and the abysmally poor and compromised response of government security agents to intimate partner violence. The Nigerian woman and

---

[19] "Divorce-Seeking Housewife Assaulted, Brutalized by Defunct SARS Officers on Husband's Instructions in Adamawa," *Sahara Reporters*, accessed December 8, 2021, www.saharareporters.com.

child seem not to be safe in their home. They are often battered, sexually abused, raped and sometimes murdered by partners or other members of family or intimate relationships.

Domestic violence can take the form of verbal, physical, economic, psychological or sexual abuse. It is so pervasive in the Nigeria society and the vulnerable suffer silently and unjustly. The assumption exists that violence against women, domestic violence and rape are private or family issues, which are not for public intervention.[20] Little wonder Lantana had to face the ire of Umar. When a victim makes recourse to the state institution (court or police, for instance) for protection and defense of their inalienable rights, it sometimes ends in a regrettably cruel narrative as evident in the case under consideration. There is the fear of victim-blaming and social stigma, especially in cases of sexual violence. A public assault in the hands of brutal and merciless government agencies is what most Nigerian women who are largely victims of familial violence are not in a hurry to suffer.

Domestic violence incidents are more reported to family members (who handle it domestically) than to the police. In the family setting where naturally headship is the prerogative of men, it is common to expect the woman to have the blame and to exonerate the male partner. Noninvolvement of the police or security agents is due to lack of faith in them and the belief that it is normal to abuse women. Emmanuel Akinade, Temitayo Adewuyi, and Afolashade Sulaiman observe that the police seem not to be well trained to receive and respond adequately to report on the phenomenon, and the

---

[20] Aihie, "Prevalence of Domestic Violence in Nigeria," 2.

country's laws relating to it are weak and obsolete.[21] Reported cases rarely have justice take its course. Rather than work for justice for the abused, the Nigerian police and courts sometimes make themselves agents of victimizers against the few women who dare to bring such supposedly private issues to the public domain as the story of Lantana reveals. One wonders how seeking court hearing for an injustice (Lantana going to court to seek for divorce) becomes a criminal offense to warrant the invitation and action of a police anti-robbery squad.

One would expect Lantana to have support from her faith community. Such hope, in the Nigerian setting, would amount to building a castle in the air. Religion in concrete terms has scarcely provided the space for believers to access resources in situations of violence against women in Nigeria.[22] Both Muslims and Christians weaponize religion to the disadvantage and marginalization of the most vulnerable. Islam makes recourse to the teaching of Mohammad as Christianity references the Scriptures and church teachings to perpetuate abuse of women and children. Seldom do preachers give sermons on domestic violence and when they did, women usually receive exhortation to behave, forgive and to make their mar-

---

[21] Emmanuel Akinade, Temitayo Adewuyi, and Afolashade Sulaiman, "Social-Legal Factors That Influence the Perpetuation of Rape in Nigeria," *Science Direct* 5 (March 2010): 1762-1763, www.sciencedirect.com.

[22] There is the inability to consider domestic violence as a problem; most religious leaders are not trained as pastoral counselors and so lack the resources; they scarcely make referrals. There are also few professional counselors.

riage and family magically work. The Nigerian woman, facing battery at home by her partner, denied protection and justice by the state, blamed and unsupported by her faith community, lives in her shell of pain and abandonment.

Both the state and church seem to serve the culture of men's subjugation of women. The social-cultural beliefs and patriarchal dominance have served to sustain domestic violence in Nigeria. Domestic violence serves to establish the authority and control of men over women in a culture that perceives women as men's subordinates. There is the morbid conception that the customary payment of bride price by the men amounts to 'purchasing' the women who becomes the husband's property. The men, as a way of disciplining erring women and children, resort to the use of force or violence.[23]

What Ought to Be Going On?

The individual person(s) rightly deserve safety, protection from the institutions and society to which they belong. They deserve their physical, mental and spiritual health to be preserved. This is the will of God for them, as he desires that we be fully alive. Battery and all forms of sexual violence against women and children dishonor the human body and constitute a violation of their human dignity and rights. In a context such as the Nigerian society where there is a high level of the various forms of domestic violence, this book envisions a church that takes the human body seriously and rises against any harm done to human beings created by God, saved by Christ and

---

[23] Aihie, "Prevalence of Domestic Violence in Nigeria," 2.

acclaimed Christ's glory.[24] Human bodies matter, and injustice or harm done to a person's body is injustice or harm done to the person. The body is a fundamental aspect of our being and, as Timothy Johnson affirms, we cannot conceive of ourselves absent from our bodies nor can we completely dispose of our bodies without at the same time losing our very selves.[25] Our body is tied to our identity. If, therefore, we are equally bodily as we are spiritual, then every human body deserves to be dignified and respected, and not violated, or ridiculed. Consequently, the Nigerian church must be ready to promote equality of men and women, old and young, and respect for the dignity and rights of all persons; she must stand tall in defense of the course of justice and empowerment of the 'least of these' brethren.[26]

Scripture tells us that God at creation made humans male and female in his own image and likeness.[27] This biblical passage provides sufficient basis for recognition of the essential equality of man and woman as human persons. Therefore, understood rightly, the relationship between men and women is not a tie of power of one over the other but a relation of complementarity, of mutual support of man and woman in respect for one another's dignity and rights. The Nigerian context, which has normalized patriarchy, subordination of women and disregard for the rights of children, yearns for a dismantling. The current situation where women and children have

---

[24] Cf Jn 17: 10 (Christian Community Bible).

[25] Timothy Luke Johnson, *The Revelatory Body: Theology as Inductive Art* (Cambridge, UK: William B. Eerdmans Publishing Co, 2015), 55.

[26] Mt 25: 40 (The New Jerusalem Bible).

[27] Gen 1:27.

the shorter end of the stick as regards certain rights and opportunities in the state is due for transformation. A situation where certain kinds of physicality are normative and others abused, sexualized and marginalized has to be condemned.

We look up to a Church that is ready and willing to confront the dominant cultural belief system that perpetuates domestic violence. This is not going to be an easy task though. For the Catholic Church in Nigeria to go about this onerous missionary task, she ought to be a church that fosters a theological anthropology that upholds the essential goodness of all humans and human flourishing. The Church is to look inward and take seriously her core functions of communion, witnessing, worship, service, preaching and teaching.[28] These traditional ministries of the Church promote the reign of God and growth of the community of faith. Such a Church community is alive to the spiritual and other needs of the faithful. A Church with this vision is concerned with and is willing therefore, "to respond to the needs of people both within and outside the faith community, [on] how to address the social structures that support or take away from human living."[29] This is the church we are called to be, in Pope Francis' ecclesiology, a" Synodal Church,"[30] that is, a listening Church,

---

[28] Thomas Groome, *Will There Be Faith? A New Vision for Educating and Growing Disciples* (New York: HarperCollins Publishers, 2011), 165-66.

[29] Jane Regan, "The Aim of Catechesis: Educating For an Adult Church," in *Horizons and Hopes: The Future of Religious Education*, ed. Thomas Groome and Harold Horell (New York: Paulist Press, 2003), 34.

[30] Synodality is focal to Pope Francis' ecclesiology. In 2021 he initiated a synodal process that involves local churches and will culminate in the

one that is attentive to the needs of the least of the brethren, standing by them in the midst of their circumstances, irrespective of how difficult or protracted this task may actually prove to be.

Domestic violence is a structure of social sin, sustained by a culture of male dominance and silence by those who can transform the status quo. We expect the Catholic Church in Nigeria to live up to the true teaching of the Church after the example of Jesus in her words and actions and so address the phenomenon of domestic violence, which impacts the lives of her vulnerable members and others in their midst.

The goal also is to see an empowering Church. A crucial way by which the Nigerian Catholic Church can address the issue of domestic violence is to empower its victims and survivors. Because of the important place of religion and spirituality in people's lives, believers look up to the church in such moments of pain and suffering. We expect neither silence nor abuse of power from the Church leaders. Their position of moral authority is considerable and recognized, and vulnerable members look up to them for hope and healing. Since the faith and community are important to most worshippers, the Church and her leaders ought to foster the emancipation of these needy members of the community.

We envision a Church where victims and survivors of familial violence receive support and resources on the trajectory to human

---

Synod of Bishops in October 2023 centering on communion, participation and mission. The central idea is ensuring a listening and participating church.

flourishing. Appropriate clergy responses make the victim of domestic violence have a feel of warmth of God's love for them and that they deserve the human flourishing that God wills for all God's children. It would be ideal for domestic violence victims to receive from their pastors and faith community the pastoral care and resources they deserve for empowerment and emancipation. As a church that has encountered a culture that marginalizes a segment of people who are God's children, it behooves the Nigerian Catholic Church to be the voice of the voiceless after Jesus who always stood for the marginalized and oppressed. The challenges facing abused women in Nigeria are urgent and require the Church's conscientious intervention. We must be present with them in the midst of the challenges they face.

Indeed, all who gather in the house of God for worship look out to experience the warmth of God's love mediated by the faithful. God is a caring and compassionate Lord and the faith community exists to make everyone have a share of this divine love. Abused persons come to worship and fellowship in their brokenness, shame, suffering, pain and despair and expect to receive solidarity, support, strength, hope to endure, and a sense of belonging. Victims and survivors of domestic violence come to church infested with wounds hoping to have the balm of Gilead applied to those wounds. The church must be ready and willing to provide the needed support and empowerment. It is by doing such heart-mending work that the church community can be true to its divine mission. Indeed, it is when congregations learn to provide practical acts of kindness, life-long compassion, hope that extends human capacity, that they experience a transformation and never remain the same again.[31]

Making the Church and Society a safe place for their most vulnerable population requires the difficult but necessary project of deconstructing the prevalent power relations that favor an understanding of power as 'power-over' others. A 'power-with' relations, which ingrains a servant-leadership model of authority creates a safe and healthy space for all especially the most vulnerable. Such subject-subject relationship does not threaten the agency of abused persons but rather fosters their emancipation and empowerment. Religious leadership will demonstrate a great leadership strength by embarking on a theology of forgiveness that goes beyond the depiction of forgiveness as cheap grace but recognizes the process of attaining forgiveness, which is repentance and the firm purpose of amendment for wrong done by the offender. This implies ensuring the accountability of perpetrators of abuse and the responsibility of bystanders. Ultimately, we envisage a synergy between church and state to ensure the defense of the dignity and rights of domestic violence survivors and victims. It is only in safe and secure environment can they heal, flourish, and be whole.

Next is a consideration of how the Nigerian context breeds domestic violence.

---

[31] Kroeger and Nason-Clark, *No Place for Abuse*, 104.

CHAPTER TWO

SOCIO-CULTURAL CONTEXT
OF DOMESTIC VIOLENCE

Where We Are

On a state visit to Berlin, Germany in 2016, a year after his election as the President of the Federal Republic of Nigeria, Muhammadu Buhari was asked, among other things, about his wife's earlier criticism of him. Aisha Buhari had said in the media that she was not going to support her husband's second-term bid unless he demonstrated that he had a grip of his government. She alarmed the control of government by a few political elite who had become more powerful than Mr. President himself had. Buhari's response to the reporter's question was shocking to many especially those from the West: "I don't know which party my wife belongs to, but she belongs to my kitchen and my living room and the other room."[32] Interestingly, Mr. Buhari, the president of the largest black nation in the world and the most populous African country, made the above nauseating and controversial comment standing on the soil of a nation governed by a woman with the Chancellor herself standing next to him. Angela Merkel (the then German Chancellor) seemed to glare at him at that instance.

---

[32] Nwachukwu Egbunike, "Nigerian President Says First Lady 'Belongs to My Kitchen' and 'The Other Room,'" *Global Voices*, October 16, 2016, https://www.globalvoices.org.

Buhari's remarks are politically incorrect, no doubt. They have attracted outrage and criticisms in the news and on social media from Nigeria and beyond. On the surface, Mr. President's statement was a retaliatory response to the sudden and unexpected attack from his wife and the First Lady in public space. Aisha in an interview with BBC's Hausa language service expressed her dissatisfaction with her husband's government. The First Lady, a businesswoman and an activist, felt that her husband had done little to fulfill his election promises to the Nigerian masses. Now Mr. President responds by ascending a public platform on the German soil to say that his wife simply belongs to the kitchen. There seems to be a political battle between the Buharis concerning their opposing perspectives on how effectively to run the Nigerian government. Mr. President seems to imagine his wife pitch tent with the opposition parties to attack his All Progressives Congress (APC) party because of his perceived incompetence. Therefore, he says, "I don't know which party she belongs to." The issue of the domestic role of Aisha (in the kitchen, bedroom and the other room) may not have arisen if the First Lady shared the same political vision with Mr. President.

A look beneath the surface however, reveals that the exchange between the President and the First Lady is more than political; it impinges on cultural matters. It unveils the crucial and critical issue of the place of women in the home and in society, and the violence that they experience in the hands of their men counterparts. Traditionally, in Nigeria women are men's subordinates. Nigeria, a country of about 200million people has over 250 ethnic groups and 500 languages. The subordination of women by men runs across these diverse cultural identities even though its severity may differ from one ethnic-cultural enclave to another. As such, in the Nigerian state, women are merely seen but not heard. This is what Mr. President tries to communicate to the world: that in Nigeria, women play the second fiddle and have no place in the public space. They are only procreators and domestic caretakers. This subordination of women by men goes with various forms of violence against women. An average Nigerian man would have no issues with Mr. President's public abuse of his wife in faraway Germany.

The highly patriarchal culture of the Nigerian society perpetuates the dominant narrative of domestic violence. This structural force (patriarchy) stems especially from some cultural and traditional beliefs that accentuate the superiority of men over women.[33] Researches indicate that Nigeria, like many Sub-Saharan African nations, has a high rate of domestic violence. Victims who are mostly women and children are battered, sexually abused, raped and sometimes murdered. Reports show that one-third and in some cases, two-thirds of women in Nigeria are victims of physical, sexual and psychological violence.[34] The result of some researchers seem to suggest that in Nigeria, every woman could expect to be a victim of one kind of violence at some point in her life, and in over 95% of domestic violence cases, men are the perpetrators.[35] Whereas the demo-

---

[33] Collins Nwabunike and Eric Tenkorang, "Domestic and Marital Violence among Three Ethnic Groups in Nigeria," *Journal of Interpersonal Violence* 32, no. 18 (2017): 2770.

[34] Aihie, "Prevalence of Domestic Violence in Nigeria," 2.

[35] Christian N. Okemgbo, Adekunbi K. Omideyi, and Clifford O. Odimegwu, "Prevalence, Patterns and Correlates of Domestic Violence in

graphic of domestic violence in Nigeria shows that the highest number of perpetrators are current husband/partner, abusers also include former husband/partner, current/former boyfriend, father/step father, mother/step mother, brother/sister, father/mother in-law, son/daughter.[36] Giving the extended family system operative in Nigeria where uncles, aunts, brothers, sisters, nephews, nieces, cousins, in-laws, and distant relatives often live in the same home, familial violence assumes a complex dynamics as it cuts across both consanguinity and affinity lines. Any male in the same household could violate females in this large family. The following observation on the dynamics of domestic violence in Nigeria is insightful:

> The society is basically patriarchal and women's place within the scheme is decidedly subordinate. Domestic violence therefore functions as a means of enforcing conformity with the role of a woman within customary society. It therefore does not matter if the woman is economically dependent or not, her position, like that of the children is subordinate.[37]

The social-cultural beliefs about women's submissiveness to men and norms that accentuate unequal socialization of the male and the female account for domestic violence across the country. The Nigerian society perpetuates this norm, by asserting normative

---

Selected Igbo Communities in Imo State, Nigeria," *African Journal of Reproductive Health* 6, no. 2 (August 2002): 102.

[36] National Population Commission, *Nigeria Demographic and Health Survey 2013* (Rockville, ML: ICF International 2014), 306.

[37] Aihie, "Prevalence of Domestic Violence in Nigeria," 2.

masculinity like supremacy and aggression with traditional norms recognizing men as family heads and breadwinners. Conversely, women keep a passive and submissive life as normative of their feminine status with procreative and domestic roles. A research on domestic violence among the three major ethnic groups in Nigeria suggests that the worldview of being a proper man or woman suggests a difference in the ways of constructing men and women in society and preserves the systemic abuse of women.[38] Traditional values, beliefs, and customs are apertures through which male domination and control are exercised and sustained.

Beginning with the coming together (union) of man and woman, the woman assumes a decidedly customary subordination that follows her all through her life in marriage and society. Among the Igbo, traditional marriage rituals involve the woman "kneeling before her prospective husband, and offering him a cup of palm wine after sipping some from the same cup herself."[39] This ritual symbolizes the woman's total submission to the man. On his part, the man pays bride price (and sundry customary material and monetary commitments) to the family of the wife-to-be. "Igbo marriage is elaborate, and a man pays a "fat" bride price or dowry, including stipulated "head drinks," and other items the kindred of the woman may demand."[40] The payment of bride price is therefore, perceived

---

[38] Nwabunike and Tenkorang, "Domestic and Marital Violence among Three Ethnic Groups in Nigeria," 2755.

[39] Nwabunike and Tenkorang, "Domestic and Marital Violence among Three Ethnic Groups in Nigeria," 2756.

[40] Nwabunike and Tenkorang, "Domestic and Marital Violence among Three Ethnic Groups in Nigeria," 2755-6.

as 'purchasing' the woman who now becomes the husband's property. It signifies "loss of rights" by the bride's family and "transfer of rights" to the groom.[41]

Stepping into her marital home, the Nigerian woman likely faces battery as a way of life. The tradition requires her to submit her whole self to her husband, and be domestically available to satisfy her spouse's physical, psychological, and sexual needs. Having bought the woman's rights, the man exhibits controlling behaviors most of the time. Manifestations of the controlling attitude include isolating the woman from her family and friends, making her too dependent on the husband and the man exhibiting a possessive mentality. Beating and coercion become means of maintaining traditional gender order and male control. As a way of disciplining erring woman and children, the male partner on his part uses battery. "[I]n beating their children, parents believe they are instilling discipline in them, much the same way as in husbands beating their wives, who like children are prone to indiscipline, which must be curbed."[42] The Nigerian woman who is perceived as not showing due respect to her husband, unfaithful, stubborn, having imposing will or lazy about doing wifely duties is bound to be disciplined. Indeed, this is the stark reality and the truth that a battered woman lives daily in the hands of an abusive male partner. She walks on eggshells, hunted by the fear of punishment if she misbehaves, and experiences the "increasing regimentation and restriction of her life in

---

[41] Nwabunike and Tenkorang, "Domestic and Marital Violence among Three Ethnic Groups in Nigeria," 2767.

[42] Aihie, "Prevalence of Domestic Violence in Nigeria," 2.

attempts to please her abusive partner, [to] placate him, and avoid being hurt again."[43] The man never gets it wrong; it is the woman all the time, and she must pay direly for it. Discipline is a means of enforcing the woman's conformity to her domestic and subservient roles in an all-men society.

Because the Nigerian society puts a high premium on procreation, the married woman who is unlucky with conception is prone to abuse not only from her husband but also from the husband's family. She is emotionally abused and battered; often the man marries another (second) wife to subjugate her further, and sometimes the woman faces threats of or actual divorce. Even pregnancy is no escape to abuse. A study of Igbo women showed that pregnant mothers were no less vulnerable to wife battery than other women were, as 58.9% of the respondents reported experiencing battery during pregnancy by their male partners.[44] The experience of violence during pregnancy has obvious health implications for the woman and has severe effects on the unborn child. When she begets only female children, the case not different. Because of the premium placed on the male child in the society, the husband and his family abuse the Nigerian woman who is unable to give birth to one (even when the fault is the husband's). Often, abuse of the Nigerian woman takes place in the presence of her children. Sometimes, children receive blows alongside their mothers. The battery of women

---

[43] Cooper-White, *The Cry of Tamar*, 126.

[44] Okemgbo, Omideyi, and Odimegwu, "Prevalence, Patterns and Correlates of Domestic Violence," 104.

and children often result to physical and emotional injuries that impact them for a long time.

Because domestic violence is not simply a single act but a pattern of behavior, battery becomes a recurring decimal. Consequently, a "cycle of violence"[45] characterizes the relationship between husband and wife. According to the cycle of violence theory, the battery relationship moves from a tension-building phase, to an acute phase and finally to the unreliable respite phase. At the tension-building phase, the victim seems to perceive danger from the batterer's attitude or disposition and strives in a variety of ways to avoid any violent incident. There is tension in the atmosphere; the victim has a feel of the tension and tries to avert the danger. The batterer strikes at the acute phase and inflicts harm on the victim. At the respite phase, the batterer uses occasional acts of kindness to soothe victim in order to keep them in abusive relationship.[46] The cycle repeats in a spiral fashion with less duration and gestures of kindness and protracted tension-building and acute phases. The respite though unreliable serves to keep the woman in the relationship when she contemplates quitting the relationship.

Again, culturally, women in Nigeria dread divorce. Marital status gives the Nigerian woman a sense of protection, relevance, honor, and safety. Divorce raises questions on the character and probity of the woman. At marriage, she loses her maiden rights and may not find her parents' house as it was; her maiden household

---

[45] Lenore Walker, a psychologist, established the "Cycle of Violence" theory. See: Cooper-White, *The Cry of Tamar*, 130.

[46] Cooper-White, *The Cry of Tamar*, 130.

now enjoys the presence and occupancy of other women married into the household who may not be friendly to her. Saying farewell to an abusive relationship is equally difficult especially when the relationship has produced offspring. The Nigerian woman would prefer to suffer any violence in the hands of her abuser for the sake of her children. For those married in the church, the fear of putting asunder what God has united is obviously deep. Unfortunately, the batterer is very much aware of these factors and thus 'weaponizes' them against the vulnerable partner. This is where we are, as unfortunate as it might be.

It will however be naïve to assume that the problem of domestic violence in Nigeria is only cultural. Colonialism has more and lasting effects on the colonized nation than can be imagined. I submit that colonialism implanted a culture of violence into the Nigerian socio-cultural fabric. British colonialism with its imperial characteristic institutionalized violence by disregarding the people's traditional leadership structure and institutions, and imposing theirs. While they met a fertile ground for indirect rule in the northern protectorate through the emirates, they imposed the indirect rule system in the southern Nigeria, which reinforced a government of control over their subjects and sometimes violated them. The institution of the Warrant Chief system in the Southeast, the Sole Native Authority system in the Southwest, and the Local Township government system in the Lagos Colony reflect the indirect rule that was imposed on people of southern Nigeria.[47] While they failed to recognize the traditional chiefs, priests and king makers who ensure checks and balances against instances of power abuse, the British in some cases dismantled local leadership structures especially where women exercised political authority.[48] The British colonial rule was male dominated and often abusive; they imposed laws and policies that were undemocratic and did not carry the locals along including taxation laws that abused women economically and led to civil conflicts.[49] The abuse of power in some cases led to the physical and sexual abuse of women like stripping women naked in the name of verifying them for taxation by their colonial stooges.[50] Colonial rule bred local leaders who become not responsive to their people's needs but to the oppressive caprices of their colonial masters. As Mercy Amba Oduyoye succinctly puts it, "Raped by the patriarchal manipulation of the (Global) North, Africa now stands in danger of further battering by home-grown patriarchies."[51]

---

[47] Mojubaolu Olufunke Okome, "Unknown Solidier: Women's Radicalism, Activism, and State Violence in Twentieth-Century Nigeria," in *Gender and Power Relations in Nigeria*, ed. Ronke Iyabowale Ako-Nai (Lanham, MD: Lexington books, 2013), 245.

[48] Okome, "Unknown Solidier," 245-46.

[49] There was the Aba Women War (1929) in the Southeast and the conflict in the Southwest that culminated in the ouster of the Alake (the traditional ruler who was perceived as the British stooge) by the community women.

[50] Okome, "Unknown Solidier," 241.

[51] Mercy Amba Oduyoye, *Daughters of Anowa: African Women and Patriachy* (Maryknoll, NY: Orbis Books, 1995), 10.

The Nigeria-Biafra war (1967-70) may also be a factor to the high rate of domestic violence Nigeria. This is following researches, which suggest a connection between the aftermath of wars, civil conflicts, political violence and domestic violence. Post-Traumatic Stress Disorder (PTSD) and depression are associated with war veterans as a study of US war veterans indicate. These mental health issues notably lead to aggressive behaviors.[52] Persons with PTSD and depression seem to experience more feelings of anger and aggression that could find expression through violence or abuse. There is every reason to believe that the civil war that ensured in less than a decade of Nigeria's independence and in which blood of millions of citizens was shed and survivors sustained mental and moral injuries is contributory to the prevalence of familial violence.

Validating the Dominant Narrative

The culture of abuse is so pervasive and dominant that the Nigerian woman becomes powerless, and in most cases, comes to accept and justify the dominant narrative. The Nigerian woman in her helplessness comes to internalize this structure of abuse. A survey carried out by UNICEF with some Nigerian women shows that 40.1% of the women (age 15-49) affirmed that their husbands could beat them either for burning food, arguing with them, going out

---

[52] S. K. Creech et al., "National Implementation of a Truama-informed Intervention for Intimate Partner Violence in the Department of Veterans Affairs: First Year Outcomes," *Health Services Research* 18, no. 1 (2018), 582.

without telling them, neglecting their children or refusing them sexual intercourse.[53] Tivs and Hausa-Fulanis justify wife beating. There is a law about "corrective beating" of women and children of Northern Nigeria (where Hausa-Fulanis mostly reside) justifying men beating their wives and children as a disciplinary measure in so far as it does not hurt.[54] 'Hurt' here refers to grave injury, which we shall expound and analyze later in chapter four. Wife beating for the Tiv ethnic people has a wide acceptance as a show of love, and consequently, it is unobjectionable to the women. A study conducted among Tiv women indicated, "more than half of ever-married women accepted and justified wife beating and hitting as a necessary male "duty" to assert manhood within the traditional family."[55] In such a scenario, one may not wonder if women exhibit certain behaviors just to attract abusive acts unto themselves.

It is not a thing of surprise that the Nigerian woman validates and internalizes this culture of violence and gender oppression. David Hooker who has done a significant work on transformative community dialogues would argue that, the dominant oppressive narrative which creates repression and social inequality limits the way the oppressed think, act, relate and perceive themselves. According to

---

[53] "Report of Domestic Violence in Nigeria," UNICEF Nigeria, accessed June 30, 2021, https://www.unicef.org/nigeria/ng_publications_nigeria_DHS_final_report.pdf.

[54] Nwabunike and Tenkorang, "Domestic and Marital Violence among Three Ethnic Groups in Nigeria," 2768.

[55] Nwabunike and Tenkorang, "Domestic and Marital Violence among three Ethnic Groups in Nigeria," 2752.

him: "When identity narratives in a community are more com-
pressed, it is likely that a person will feel more constrained in their
behaviors."[56] The Nigerian woman is born in this dominant margin-
alizing culture, lives it and, transmits it to her children. For many, it
is difficult to realize or accept the reality of their abuse. They are
born in it, bathed in it, breathe it and schooled in it. Consequently,
reporting rate is low as the abused accept it as normal and there is
little or no effort toward emancipation by the abused.

The research of Collins Nwabunike and Eric Tenkorang on domestic and marital violence among the three major ethnic groups in
Nigeria (Igbo, Yoruba, and Hausa) indicate that the Igbo women experience the highest level of physical, emotional and sexual violence
and the Hausa women coming least. The study, which presents the
ethnic dimension of domestic violence in Nigeria, concludes that
Igbo men are most abusive and patriarchal.[57] One way to understand
the high rate of familial violence Igboland is from the perspective of
the Civil War aforementioned. This was the province where the war
was fought, and all who lived in the area were casualties of war.

Considering other factors, one can also argue that while it is true
that domestic violence differs from one local culture to another (war
being a likely factor), what determines the variation is not simply a
matter of less male dominance by menfolk of any ethnic group. I

---

[56] David A. Hooker, *The Little Book of Transformative Community
Conferencing: A Hopeful, Practical Approach to Dialogue* (New York: Good
Books, 2016), 35.

[57] Nwabunike and Tenkorang, "Domestic and Marital Violence among
three Ethnic Groups in Nigeria," 2767.

argue that the basis of the variance is more about the level of acceptability of the dominant narrative by women. This is for obvious factors. The Hausa women are predominantly Muslim, and Islam, a religion that accentuates submission, makes true its tenet of submission to the will of Allah and in corollary, the women's submission to men's whims and caprices. Most Muslim women in Nigeria have low socioeconomic status (SES) and are uneducated,[58] following the dominant Nigerian Islamic school that favors uneducated, fully veiled, and secluded women.[59] They also have high cases of forced and early marriages (often marriage of minors), and are least empowered. The Igbo and Yoruba women who are more educated and read suffer more frequent abuse as their efforts to express their agency unfortunately meet their husbands' aggression. The Nigeria Demographic and Health Survey shows that women with no education are less likely to experience physical and sexual violence.[60]

Other intimate relationships between men and women follow similar abusive traits or pattern. Boyfriends batter their girlfriends as men abuse their concubines. These kinds of relationships are likely to be more abusive. In the Nigerian society, such intimacies are usually secret and informal, and as such, the womenfolk are

---

[58] Nwabunike and Tenkorang, "Domestic and Marital Violence among three Ethnic Groups in Nigeria," 2768.

[59] Balaraba Sule and Priscilla Starratt, "Islamic Leadership Positions for Women in Contemporary Kano State," in *Hausa Women in the Twentieth Century*, ed. Catherine Coles and Beverly Mack (Madison: The University of Wisconsin Press, 1991), 31-32.

[60] National Population Commission, *Nigeria Demographic and Health Survey 2013*, 304, 307.

more likely to bear the scores of the resulting dehumanization in silence. Women in such relationships keep hoping that things would get better as the intimacy grows. In the end, all they experience is a circle of violence. Sometimes, they live with it because it is a temporary or secondary relationship, and other times due to the material benefit.

It would be naïve to imagine that woman are incapable of cruelty and meanness. There are instances where women abuse their male partners. The percentage is low however, as our discussion so far has indicated. Nevertheless, we can explain such display of power as more or less the reaction of helplessness of one whose back is against the wall. Women who abuse their male partners often do so due to the unbearable battery of the latter and sometimes as self-defense. Pamela Cooper-White describes such instances as reactionary and mostly unconscious. According to her:

Women who verbally abuse frequently do so out of a context of relative powerlessness, which they do not consciously recognize. In the absence of genuine equality and affirmation of their self-worth, women sometimes do resort to the tactics of the oppressed: manipulation, hypercriticism, contemptuous speech and body language, or nagging. These strategies ultimately do not solve anything, but may fulfill a victim's (mostly unconscious) need simply to do something in order to maintain some sense of agency.[61]

---

[61] Cooper-White, *The Cry of Tamar*, 133.

While one may argue about cases of abusive women that are more than reactionary, such instances are infinitesimal compared in ratio to men's abusive behavior toward women. Abuse takes a variety of forms and constitutes a violation of the basic rights of humans irrespective of gender.

CHAPTER THREE

FORMS AND EFFECTS OF DOMESTIC VIOLENCE

Domestic violence could be physical, emotional, sexual, economic or spiritual and impacts the victim (bodily, mentally or spiritually), family, church and society adversely.

Physical Violence

As aforementioned, every woman in Nigeria has likely suffered one form of violence or another at some point in her life. In the home and in other intimate relationships, the Nigerian woman is violated physically. Physical violence is a very common form of domestic violence. It is the use of physical force on persons to the extent that injures them or puts them at risk of being injured. Physical abuse involves beating, slapping, kicking, knocking, punching, choking, and confinement.[62] The injury inflicted with masculine hands is often as severe as that perpetrated with hard objects. Some men are so brutal and aggressive that they use any available object to inflict injury on the woman or child. Such objects include (but not limited to) machetes, axes and acid. Machete cutting and acid bath of vulnerable women are not uncommon in the Nigerian context. The injuries inflicted by these objects range from minor to major injuries that may disfigure victim's body. The abused person bears

---

[62] Aihie, "Prevalence of Domestic Violence in Nigeria," 3.

so much suffering and pain. The disfigurement resulting from injuries and emotional suffering of such cruelty by so-called lover is better experienced than imagined.

Sometimes, domestic violence results in the death of victim. In their account of the prevalence of the phenomenon in Nigeria, Christian Okemgbo, Adekunbi Omideyi, and Clifford Odimegwu cited cases of physical violence that resulted in the death of their victims. They reported the case of a 12-year-old woman who met her premature death after she had her both legs amputated by her spouse with an axe after she repeatedly ran away from him (perchance, in an attempt to escape abuse). Equally mentioned were about five cases of the use of women's bodies for rituals and the incident where a man burnt his wife alive because of an argument between them in the course of which he accused his wife of raining insults on him and his family. Finally, the authors cited the case of the murder of a nursing mother slaughtered in her sleep by her husband who claimed to be under the influence of supernatural powers.[63] Not long ago, a man killed his wife by kicking her in the chest. The deceased, a popular Nigerian gospel musician who wanted to save her marriage for obvious reasons, met her sudden death in a hospital after suffering from blood clot following battery from her abusive husband.[64] Earlier on, a man beat his wife to death for refusing him sex in a city in the southern part of the country. Emmanuel

---

[63] Okemgbo, Omideyi, and Odimegwu, "Prevalence, Patterns and Correlates of Domestic Violence," 102.

[64] Onu Stephen, "Osinachi Nwachukwu Brutalized by Husband before her Death – Singer Alleges" *Premium Times* (Nigeria), April 9, 2022 and "Pastors Begged "Ekweme" Singer, Osinachi to Return Home after she left

Asemota murdered his wife, Ugieki Asemota, on June 28, 2021 in her room at their residence.[65] The frequency of death cases is high but underreported in the media. As horrendous and heinous as these crimes are, often the perpetrators walk into their houses and sleep with their two eyes closed. The assumption is that domestic violence is a private matter; the man has long bought the woman as a property by the marriage contract. At best, if the woman's maiden family has what it takes, as in the case of Ugieki Asemota, they could push the matter to the public space. Often, the justice system treats it with levity or dismiss it after collecting bribes from the culprit.

Physically abusing the woman's or the child's body is a terrible form of dehumanization. It is a great dishonor to the human body created in God's image and likeness. It is a grave human abuse, a violation of victim's dignity and rights. It is as if being a woman is a crime. Violence against women robs them of their dignity and humanity. It demeans and denigrates their personhood and constitutes a damage to our common human nature. How good it would serve the Nigerian state and church to realize that such gender-based violence is a violation of basic human rights and an attack on our common humanity.

Abusive Marriage – Mother of late Gospel Singer," *Sahara Reporters* (New York), April 12, 2022.

[65] Oluwatosin Omojuyibe, "Man beats wife to death for refusing sex in Edo," *The Punch Newspaper* (Nigeria), July 14, 2021.

Sexual Abuse

The cruelest manifestation of masculinity is the sexual abuse of the Nigerian woman. Whereas she is assigned by the culture to gratify her husband's sexual needs, she faces coercion whenever she is not able to play this expected role for whatever reasons. Sexual abuse could come in the form of sexual assault, stalking, harassment or exploitation. It includes the coercion of a person to engage in sexual relations, marital rape, and getting children involved in sexual activities such as child prostitution/trafficking and pornography. The male partner employs intimidation to instill fear in her. Threats, coercion and masculinity all serve to subdue the woman and force her into sexual acts against her will. Often, it happens that the Nigerian adult woman survived abuse as a child and so may only have a vague understanding of her safety rights or what constitutes a loving relationship. In this case, she confuses love with the abuse she experienced earlier in life. The one who was lucky to have had no experience of child abuse but finds herself in an abusive relationship, finds herself taken aback by the reality of violence in her adult relationship.

The girl child seldom voices out the experience of sexual violation by an adult. This is more so when a family member, teacher or someone their parents know and respect perpetuates the abuse. Because developmentally, the child, prior to adolescence cannot imagine a worldview other than their parents', it is difficult to distinguish good from bad relationships. Thus, in cases of sexual assault, the likely response of the child is that of what Roland Summit calls

'Child Sexual Accommodation Syndrome.'[66] The child experiences the feeling of secrecy, helplessness, entrapment, accommodation. The threat and coercion from the abuser about the consequences of disclosure reinforce the child's helplessness to keep the incest secret. Again, the child rarely resists physically, out of confusion, guilt, secrecy, self-sense of powerlessness, dependency, and of course often out of love for the perpetrator. [67] Fear and the dismissal of her story as phantom in the face of abuse confront the adolescent. The Nigerian adolescent female is stuck in the prevailing culture of sexual secrecy and privacy. UNICEF Nigeria reports that every year, over nine million children under the age of eighteen have exposure to sexual violence in Nigeria. One out of every four girls and one out of every ten boys experience sexual abuse. These children are stalked, harassed, forced or pressured to have sex or experience attempted sex.[68]

At workplace, the woman finds herself coerced into 'quid pro quo' harassment. Her sexual compliance to her employer becomes a condition for hiring or firing her and used to make such decisions that concern her work and entitlements like remuneration, promotion and job allocation. Today, in both public and private sectors, it is not enough for someone to get a job, gain promotion or attract a contract by bribery alone. Bribery may pave way for the man but not

---

[66] Roland Summit, "The Child Sexual Abuse Accommodation Syndrome," *Attachment: New Directions in Psychology and Relational Psychoanalysis* 7, no.2 (July 2013): 129-136.

[67] Cooper-White, *The Cry of Tamar*, 171.

[68] "Child Sexual Abuse in Nigeria," UNICEF Nigeria, accessed July 5, 2021, www.unicefnigeria.org.

for the woman. Besides paying her way through, often the woman has to go the sexual route. The Nigerian woman is also exposed to 'hostile environment' harassment in which case her work is unreasonably interfered with, a situation that creates an intimidating, offensive and hostile working space and consequently impacts her performance. Unfortunately, the structure of the society is such that it does not guarantee the safety of women as the culture of accountability and justice is a desideratum.

The Nigerian woman equally suffers sexual harassment and assault in the hands of her landlord, husband's kin and friends. This happens especially to the widow, separated or divorced woman. Culturally, the man shields the woman from the coercion of the male-dominated society. A man tends to protect the woman against the marauding of the rampaging men who prey on women to satisfy their sexual needs (besides their wives- in case of married men). The married man who wants to avoid sex with wife (especially the one whose wife is pregnant or has reached menopause) tends to look out for other women to gratify his sexual needs. The widow, separated or divorced woman becomes an endangered species. Thus, she is more likely to experience sexual violence than her married and never-married counterparts are.[69]

In its various forms and circumstances, sexual violence is very devastating and degrading. It is particularly difficult to account for it or report it as the woman is usually reluctant to tell her story. Sex,

---

[69] National Population Commission, *Nigeria Demographic and Health Survey 2013*, 305.

in the Nigerian context, is sacred; seldom are sexual relations especially violent instances shared with others. Sexual violation is overwhelming, involves the sense of guilt, shame and victim blaming
that very often the victim prefers to handle personally despite its
emotional scourge. The trauma seems to be re-lived by sharing (as
people would either blame you or be unwilling to support you), and
the fear of not being believed is dreaded. Sexual abuse erodes the
woman's confidence, stifles her initiative and devastates her emotional and physical health. In its various forms, sexual violation in-
vades one of the profoundest and most intimate boundaries of a
woman's sense of self.

Emotional Abuse

We cannot overlook the emotional or psychological abuse that
the Nigerian woman suffers. She is exposed constantly to name-call-
ing, undue criticism, intimidation, exploitation, humiliation and
threats from her male partner. She is made to feel bad about herself
and is subjected to social isolation. Isolation reinforces the woman's
entrapment and the batterer's dominance. Gradually, the batterer
undermines the woman's family, friends and loved ones. He leads
the victim to disengage emotionally with relationships the victim
had hitherto and to begin to buy into his isolating worldview. Intimidation instills fear in the victim and disempowers them. Mr. President, by intimidating his wife in Berlin disempowered her and made
her to redress her activist and emancipatory campaigns. When on
June 4, 2021, Mr. President banned the use of Twitter by the Nigerian population, a policy greeted with condemnation by Nigerians

(at home and in the diaspora) and people around the world, Aisha, in faraway Dubai deactivated her Twitter handle in solidarity with her husband.[70] She has been cowed to be silent over her husband's corrupt government and for long learned to suppress her critical guts.

In the home and in abusive relationships, the abused partner is rendered powerless and coerced to subdue their resistance and assertiveness. In the end, their sense of self-worth is impacted and they are at the danger of having severe behavioral, cognitive, emotional or mental problems. Children who witness domestic violence experience psychological abuse.

Economic Abuse

To perfect his total domination of the woman, the abusive partner insists on making his spouse a housewife. In this way, she would be economically dependent on him. Economic abuse also includes stealing from or defrauding the victim, refusing to provide her money required for necessities such as food and medical treatment, manipulating or exploiting her for financial gain or controlling her choice of work. Under the above circumstances, the Nigerian woman is compelled to depend totally on the partner for practically everything including her personal effects. The man controls what comes in and what goes out. He makes the major decisions. When

---

[70] "Dubai-based Nigerian First Lady, Aisha Buhari Deactivates Twitter Account in Solidarity with Husband," *Sahara Reporters* (New York), June 4, 2021, www.sharareporters.com.

she has the opportunity to work, her spouse controls her finances. The victim can only but do the predator's bidding. She is a stranger in her own house, having access to limited resources as provided and often not aware of the man's business.

Spiritual Abuse

The Nigerian woman is arguably religious. In good times, she enjoys offering praises to God before her worshipping community. In bad times, she frequents the house of God like the biblical Hannah to pour her tears and grief before her maker and refuge. Researches show people's faith or spirituality impact their coping ability or their well-being. Some of these researches suggest that a religious transformation may be an important resource for coping with lifetime traumatic experience such as domestic violence. Marie Fortune argues that, like any other crisis, domestic violence victims experience a crisis of meaning in their lives. Confronted with an experience of domestic violence, a person's religious beliefs and community of faith can serve as a primary support system to the individual and his/her family.[71] It is not surprising then that the Nigerian woman frequents the church and faith community fellowship to deal with life and familial challenges. Even in doing so, she faces

---

[71] Marie Fortune, "The importance of Religion and Faith" in *Walking Together: Working with Women from Diverse Religious and Spiritual Traditions, A Guide for Domestic Violence Advocates,* ed. Jean Anton (Seattle: Faith Trust Institute, 2005), 11-12.

spiritual abuse. This occurs in the form of preventing her from engaging in her spiritual or religious practices, punished by an abusive partner for participating in religious or church activities. The abusive and domineering male partner is suspicious and afraid of her association with others less she tells her story and/or learns to resist or question his abusive behavior. Isolation becomes a handy tool for the abuser.

Spiritual abuse may also take the form of using one's religious belief to manipulate, dominate or control the victim. Often, Scripture serves as a tool to disable and disempower women. The Christian men are swift to cite Scripture to buttress women's subordination to them. They are quick to remind their wives that the woman was gotten from the man's ribs (Gen 2:21-22) and that the wife should be obedient or subservient to her husband (Eph 5:22). How can they realize that from the beginning, they were created equal (Gen 1:27-28) and that husband and wife owe each other mutual submission out of reverence for Christ (Eph 5:21)? The frequently referenced biblical passage is 1 Peter 3:1-6 that speaks about wives' submission to their husbands. The average Nigerian man expects that his partner should bear the unfair suffering and pain of abuse with patience and resignation. The scriptural coloration and coating heightens the violence. It however suffices to state that while one may undertake to suffer for one's faith, suffering battery at the hands of an abusive partner is unjust and non-redemptive. Abuse 'in the name of God' does no good to victimizer, victim or bystander including children. Instead, the damaging effect of abuse to the abuser, victim and the family is enormous. Domestic violence turns the home into a war zone. Indeed, abused women are "prisoners of war as any captured soldier, except that no one knows to look for them, and often no one will believe their stories if they tell."[72]

Consequences of Domestic Violence

Who would experience any form of the abuses mentioned above and remain ever the same? Every kind of abuse has its dire effects on its victim, the family and society at large. Violence impacts the entire being- body, mind and soul; it constitutes a serious public health issue. It affects the internal human bodily and mental mechanisms as well as the individual's relation to the world beyond the self. Domestic violence is an infringement on victim's dignity, human rights, societal freedom, and reproductive health. The body as created by God is sacred and worthy of honor. Domestic violence is an abuse, violation, discrimination, marginalization of the human body or person. The Christian anthropology affirms the goodness that is inherent in all humans as creatures of God, created in God's goodness and likeness. This goodness imbues us with dignity and respect. Sadly, familial violence dishonors the body, robs victims of their dignity and humanity. Jesus said, "I have come that they may have life and have it abundantly."[73] The fullness of life promised by Our Lord begins by honoring the body even as he did during his earthly life and ministry. Battery, isolation, and sexual assault of a woman are awful expressions of masculinity and a violation of the selfhood of the victim. They constitute a tremendous injury to women. Violence against

---

[72] Cooper-White, *The Cry of Tamar*, 130.

[73] Jn 10:10.

women impacts their freedom of choice, their integrity, and their dignity; it is a denial of community and a distortion of right relationships.[74]

The physical health issues associated with domestic violence are enormous. Victims (be they children or adults) may sustain bodily injuries like minor cuts, scratches and bruises. The injuries may be more serious and may include long-term disabilities such as broken bones, internal bleeding, head injuries or trauma, and lacerations.[75] These are acute effects of the phenomenon and require medical attention and hospitalization. Sometimes, due to poverty, fear or secrecy, victims are unable to access the medical assistance they need to deal with these health concerns. Because abusive behavior is not just a one-instance act but rather a repeated occurrence, victims may become weary of seeking required medical attention. Arthritis and irritable bowel syndrome are among the chronic health conditions associated with victims of familial violence. Whereas, abused pregnant women experience greater risk of miscarriage, pre-term labor, and injury to or death of the unborn child.[76] The health risks that arise from sexual abuse include sexually transmitted diseases (STDs), and teenage pregnancies. Abortion becomes an option for some in instances of pregnancy. Because of the persistent secrecy associated with sex, and sometimes due to pressure from perpetrators, the poor teenager often patronizes patent medicine dealers or quack

---

[74] Mai-Anh Le Tran, *Reset the Heart: Unlearning Violence, Relearning Hope* (Nasville: Abingdon, 2017), 24.

[75] Fareo Oluremi, "Domestic Violence against Women in Nigeria," *European Journal of Psychological Research* 2, no.1 (2015): 28.

[76] Oluremi, "Domestic Violence against Women in Nigeria," 28.

doctors who complicate issues and compromise victim's reproductive health and fertility, which sometimes lead to their premature death. Even many health facilities in the country are inefficient and poorly equipped to provide the required medical support. In all, domestic violence raises the rate of morbidity and mortality in women in Nigeria.

The emotional and psychological harm done to the Nigerian woman and child are more acute and devastating. Domestic abuse affects the general functionality and interpersonal relationships of victim. They often exhibit low self-esteem and difficulty to trust others. Sexual abuse especially affects the way they trust others (may be too little or too much trust), the nuances and quality of trust as well as the readiness to trust people in any relationship. The Nigerian child exposed to abuse is likely to experience symptoms of Post-Traumatic Stress Disorder (PTSD). These include depression, nightmares, and other sleep problems, vague feelings of anxiety and dread, a constant sense of being on guard, difficulties with trust and intimacy, uncontrolled outburst of temper, and problems with sexual relating and with forming healthy relationships in general.[77] Nigeria is yet to take the mental health of her citizens seriously and have scarce mental health personnel and facilities. Victims of emotional or psychological abuse often end up suffering without appropriate attention.

Furthermore, the child who witnesses abuse or lives in an environment where some other person, for the most part a caregiver, is a victim of abuse can have disastrous psychological problems. The

---

[77] Cooper-White, *The Cry of Tamar*, 179.

child could experience learning and cognitive disorders by exposure to abusers and spousal abuse. According to Lundy Bancroft, any of the following psychological symptoms could be manifest in children exposed to domestic violence: attention deficits, hyperactivity that interferes with learning and attention, learning delays, delays in language acquisition, poor academic performance, missing school often through sickness or truancy, falling asleep in school, sibling rivalry or hierarchy. While Bancroft indicates that the above behaviors are not limited to witnessing domestic violence, he states that exposure to an abuser causes children to be manipulated easily, suffer traumatic bonding, and become involved in undermining their mother.[78]

Whether the child witnesses domestic violence or is victimized by it, it raises a health concern and leaves them with severe physical, behavioral and emotional problems that often affect them in adolescent and adult life. The research of Cindy Sousa et al, concluded that children exposed to domestic violence and child abuse are at a higher risk of having antisocial behaviors in their adolescent life.[79] Socialized in violent and harmful health behaviors like excessive smoking, alcohol abuse, use of drugs and engagement in risky sexual activity, the child becomes a danger to self and to others. In the end,

---

[78] Lundy Bancroft, *When Dad Hurts Mom: Helping your Children Heal the Wounds of Witnessing Abuse* (New York: Putnam, 2004), 76, 145-46.

[79] Cindy Sousa et al., "Longitudinal Study on the Effects of Child Abuse and Children's Exposure to Domestic Violence, Parent-Child Attachments, and Antisocial Behavior in Adolescence," *Journal of Interpersonal Violence* 26, no.1, (2011): 128.

what we get is the destruction of the individual and their immediate environment.

Among the numerous consequences of intimate partner violence is the fact that its victims often find themselves in a position of dependence - financial, emotional, or physical. Abuse suppresses the agency of abused persons. They are often stuck in the relationship and in a life of dependence. When they finally leave their abuser, victims are overwhelmed with the reality of the extent to which the abuse has muzzled their autonomy. They usually have little or no money of their own or persons on whom they can rely when they need assistance. A major challenge that confronts women in abusive relationships is the economic factor and it is so overwhelming that many women end up staying in those relationships. To crown it all, victims of domestic violence often do not have the specialized skills, education, and training that would otherwise help them get meaningful jobs; some may have several children to provide for.[80]

For many women, domestic violence disrupts their understanding of marriage; it could also affect their experience of faith community and relationship with God. A joyous spontaneity and a life of shared joys and sorrows characterize Christian marriage. Domestic violence disrupts this understanding as a partner now inflicts suffering and pain on his spouse. Thus, the appropriation of the lament of the psalmist by the abused: "Were it an enemy that taunted me, that I could bear; if an opponent pitted against me, I could turn away from him. But you, a person of my own rank, a comrade and a dear friend, to whom I was bound by intimate friendship in the house of

---

[80] Oluremi, "Domestic Violence against Women in Nigeria," 28.

God."[81] Intimate partner violence is a betrayal of trust. It destroys the love and respect of married life. It is a destruction of the balance and spontaneity of the relationship, which brings obstruction of effective prayer as well as true communion in marriage. A mistrust of this divine institution affects victims' perception of faith community and relationship with God. Ultimately, abused persons face disorientation. Their God-given energy and talents are dissipated in trying to avoid violence and in wanting to gratify their insatiable partners. In the end, the society and her constitutive institutions are affected.

---

[81] Ps 55: 12-14.

CHAPTER FOUR

THE NIGERIAN STATE AND DOMESTIC VIOLENCE

Though they vowed to be our safeguards

As part of global measures to secure the rights of women in modern society, the UN held a convention of member countries in 1979 known as the Convention on Elimination of all Forms of Discrimination Against Women (CEDAW). According to the convention, member states shall take every adequate measures to change the social and cultural patterns of conduct for men and women in order to attain the elimination of prejudices, customary and all other practices rooted in the idea of inferiority or superiority of either of the sexes or on the stereotyped roles for men and women.[82] Nigeria was one of the participating nations at the convention, which the UN General Assembly adopted as an international bill of rights for women. Worthy of mention is that Nigeria is one of the 186 countries that as at 2010 have ratified the convention's treaty. Also ratified by the Nigerian state are the Declaration on Violence Against Women (1993) and Protocol to the African Charter on Human and People's Rights on the Rights of Women in Africa (2003) which are equally human rights treaties that promote the rights of women.

By ratifying the treaties, Nigeria has a legal obligation to observe and promote the terms of these treaties and not to undermine the

---

[82] Dubravka Simonovic, "Convention on Elimination of all Forms of Discrimination Against Women," United Nations, accessed July 8, 2021, https://www.un.org.

protection of the rights secured by them. The question is, has the outcome of the ratification of these treaties made any major impact on the life of Nigerian women and girl-children? It may be interesting to know that more than four decades after the CEDAW and close to two decades after the African Charter, there are no available national statistics on domestic or gender violence by the Nigerian government or her agencies. The only available data come from the reports or documentations of Non-Governmental Organizations (NGOs). The scenario reinforces the assumption that Nigeria as a nation is yet to regard domestic violence as a problem. This creates two significant problems. "It also prevents law enforcement agencies from allocating time and resources for tackling the problem and recognizing it as a crime. It also makes it impossible to determine if cases of gender violence have reduced or increased."[83] There is thus, a fundamental problem, that of inability to recognize domestic violence as a crime. This single factor is largely responsible for the prevalence of the phenomenon in the Nigerian society. Again, it becomes difficult to have the demographic or to assess the situation hence batterers have their field day.

The lack of the consideration of domestic violence as a serious issue by the Nigerian state reflects in her policies. The question of the fate of the Nigerian women following the ratified treaties will be determined largely by considering what policies the state has put in place to secure their rights. Has the government enacted any policy on gender violence following the conventions? Neither the military

---

[83] Osai Ojigho, "Prohibiting Domestic Violence through Legislation in Nigeria," *Agenda*, no. 82 (2009): 87.

nor the civilian administrations after the conventions were involved in a policy to honor the ratified treaties or to respond to the urgency that the phenomenon of familial violence deserves. Thus, following the CEDAW (and other treaties) ratification, "there is no government policy on gender in- equality in Nigeria and there is a lack of awareness on the part of the populace especially those affected by gender inequality."[84] The documentation of evidence of violence against women in the country is recent and consequently, only scarce epidemiological research has a record of its frequency and myriad effects. As mentioned earlier, independent bodies or NGOs made the documentation.

Participation in and ratification of international or foreign treaties is one thing and their incorporation into the national legal system (or making policies concerning them) is yet another for a country like Nigeria. Nigeria, like most former British colonies, operates on a system that limits the effect of a treaty ratified by the state until the state's law-making body domesticates it. This principle (otherwise known as Transformation or Blackstonian doctrine) stipulates that a treaty require another legal protocol by the legislature in order to have an effect of law in the state. Section 12(1) of the 1999 Constitution of the Federal Republic of Nigeria mirrors the Transformation doctrine with the provision that: "No treaty between the Federation and any other country shall have the force of law except to the extent to which any such treaty has been enacted into law by

---

[84] Okemgbo, Omideyi, and Odimegwu, "Prevalence, Patterns and Correlates of Domestic Violence," 113.

the National Assembly."[85] The implication is that any foreign policy or treaty ratified by the Nigerian state would necessarily pass through an internal legislative process before considering it as a binding statue in the country. What this means is that until the National Assembly is able to domesticate the treaties that forbid domestic violence, these treaties are not enforceable in the Nigerian society. The National Assembly is yet to enact a law to incorporate the treaties and does not seem to be ready to do so. As we mentioned in chapter one, the legislature is resisting every effort by the Nigerian women both from inside and outside its chambers to pass the Gender Equality Bill or any women related bill. This leaves one with no doubt that domestic violence, despite its prevalence in the nation, is not a priority to the government or at least a matter in the bottom of their list.

The Fate of Abused Victims before the State Legal System

Confronted with such legal insensitivity, victims of domestic violence only have the choice of relying on criminal or civil provisions of the Nigerian constitution in seeking for justice. Section 34(1) (a) of the constitution states that "every individual is entitled to respect for the dignity of person, and accordingly- no person shall be subject to torture or to inhuman or degrading treatment."[86] Domestic violence has no specific mention here. Osai Ojigho, a Nigerian legal

---

[85] "Nigeria's Constitution of 1999 with Amendments Through 2011," *Constitute,* https://www.constituteproject.org.

[86] "Nigeria's Constitution of 1999 with Amendments Through 2011," *Constitute.*

practitioner, human rights expert, and gender equality advocate highlights how the Nigerian legal system makes no room for victims of intimate partner violence. The administration of criminal justice in Nigeria, she explains, is through two jurisdictions: Northern (predominantly Muslim) and Southern (predominantly Christian) Nigeria. The two main statutes are the Penal Code[87] (which reflects the sharia legal system) and the Criminal Code[88] (that mirrors common law) for the northern and southern regions respectively. Following the Islamic tradition, Section 55(1) (d) of the Penal Code states that husbands are allowed to punish their wives provided it is permitted by their native custom and it does not result to 'grievous hurt'. Grievous hurt in this case as defined in section 241 of the Penal Code includes "but not limited to, loss of one eye, facial disfiguration and loss of a limb."[89] Depending on whether the assailant was provoked and whether he makes use of dangerous weapon, punishment for the perpetrator ranges from a fine or four years to fourteen years of

---

[87] The Penal Code came into force on September 30, 1960 (penultimate the October 1, 1960 independence of the country) in the Northern Nigeria, a region that is predominantly Muslim.

[88] The Nigerian Criminal Code derives from Nigeria Criminal Code Act of 1916, Nigeria Penal Code Act and other criminal laws enacted by the Parliament from time to time. It essentially English criminal law and applies to the Southern region of the country that is predominantly Christian.

[89] Ojigho, "Prohibiting Domestic Violence through Legislation in Nigeria," 88.

incarceration.[90] The implication is that the Nigeria Muslim woman would wait to lose her eye or limb before her abuser could be held accountable for the harm done to her. This is only if she would not be accused of provoking the perpetrator, a clause contained in the Penal Code that would vindicate the latter.

There is no reference made in the Criminal Code about domestic violence. In talking about punishment for criminal assault on persons, the Code regrettably makes discriminatory provisions based on gender of the victim. According to section 353 of the Criminal Code, an assault is a felony, which attracts three years imprisonment, and in section 360 of the Criminal Code, indecent assault of a female is a misdemeanor and only involves a maximum of two years imprisonment. It is obvious that the provisions of the law do not fairly deal with familial violence as a phenomenon with the seriousness that it deserves. Ojigho concludes, and rightly so, that: "The problem is that the Penal Code reinforces the notion that men have authority over women since the beating of a woman, in order to correct her, is considered permissible. The cultural and religious settings in Nigeria make it difficult for women to speak out about violence."[91]

In chapter two, we noted that the prevalence of domestic violence in Nigeria is predicated predominantly on the socio-cultural context of the Nigerian society. Its patriarchal structure is such that the phenomenon serves to establish the authority of men over the

---

[90] Ojigho, "Prohibiting Domestic Violence through Legislation in Nigeria," 88.

[91] Ojigho, "Prohibiting Domestic Violence through Legislation in Nigeria," 88.

womenfolk. This worrisome scenario is worsened further by a deficient criminal justice system, which is insensitive to the suffering and pain of women and the girl-children resulting from gender-based violence. It is difficult for the law enforcement agencies to treat domestic violence as a criminal act. The government system reinforces the cultural and customary belief that domestic violence is not for public domain and as such decline to prosecute. Consequently, there is a mistrust of the system. This lack of faith in the judicial system and law enforcement agencies shuts victims out from seeking redress. Hence, the underreporting of cases of domestic violence in the Nigerian society.[92] Indeed, many victims (especially of sexual violence) keep mute for fear of reprisal from victimizers, social stigma, victim blaming or the belief that reporting to the police and the judicial system would make no difference. The scenario is that police usually dismiss reports of marital violence brought to them as a 'private matter'[93] and as such not meant for public intervention.

Furthermore, the cost of litigation in Nigeria is high. The average Nigerian woman who struggles to provide herself (and her children) with the necessities of life even when she is determined to pursue her case legally may not afford this expensive endeavor. As part of the litigation cost, she has to pay for contracting attorney(s) throughout the process. Again, the legal process is long usually with unpredictable delays between the time of listing and trying cases in court. The procedures for bringing an action in court are complex

---

[92] Aihie, "Prevalence of Domestic Violence in Nigeria," 3.

[93] Aihie, "Prevalence of Domestic Violence in Nigeria," 3.

and abused women refrain from bringing criminal actions against their abusers. The courts are formal institutions guided by complex and technical procedures, which non-legal practitioners may not comprehend. Meanwhile, the forms used in court processes are not written in simple grammar for the good understanding of the average Nigerian woman.[94]

This scenario discourages victims from choosing the legal option. The agony and frustration of the Nigerian woman is deep as the state captains she elected to protect her fundamental rights rather abuse those rights. Besides, the Nigerian state lacks resources for victims and survivors of domestic violence. No shelters or places of refuge for victims whose houses have become war zones. Thus, the abused Nigerian woman carries her life daily in her hands and wonders from where shall come her help as those she elected into power cannot vouch for her safety and inviolable rights.

The truth of the matter is that the phenomenon is not only about the rights of women, it is largely about the welfare of society. This is point that the protesters at the National Assembly (mentioned in chapter one) and advocates of gender equality try to put across. Perhaps the Nigerian society and her leaders might reconsider their attitude to domestic violence if they see it from the prism of the harm it does to the state and her constitutive institutions. The words of Lisa Fontes are insightful. In an interview she granted to UMass

---

[94] Ojigho, "Prohibiting Domestic Violence through Legislation in Nigeria," 88.

Magazine after the publication of her book: *Invisible Chains: Overcoming Coercive Control in Your Intimate Relationship,* the professor of Psychology has this to say:

> Think of it this way: society's being deprived of the talents of these people who are spending all their time worrying about pleasing their abuser instead of being able to work, contribute to their communities or raise their children freely. Sometimes, they are even committing crimes for their abuser. Coercive control causes people to drop out, because they are not free anymore to pursue their own goals or their education. Violence against women is also a cause of child abuse and neglect. It's in the state's best interest to ensure women are free.[95]

Domestic violence becomes a sort of brain drain, which stifles society of her endowed talents at the altar of androcentricism. The state has indeed failed the womenfolk. What about the church and other religious bodies?

---

[95] Lisa Fontes, "Power Play," *UMass Magazine* (Boston), Fall 2017 (Interview granted by Laura Marjorie Miller).

CHAPTER FIVE

THE CHURCH'S RESPONSE TO DOMESTIC VIOLENCE

The Church: The Last Beacon of Hope?

Religion constitutes and exacts so great an influence on people and nations than is often recognized. Charles Kimball, a professor of comparative religion, acknowledges the tremendous power of the phenomenon on humans and society when he asserts that "religion is arguably the most powerful and pervasive force on human society."[96] The Church, a religious institution, is central to the Nigerian community and constitutes a powerful force in the life and activities of the Nigerian woman. The African communalistic culture is very much lived in the church community setting as worshippers gather in worship and praise of God and in solidarity with one another. The Nigerian woman brings her whole being in an admirable fashion to an amazing embodying liturgy. Meanwhile, it is often the default of believers to run or cry to God when the storm of life strikes. They usually turn to their church when seeking for a job, trying to cope with job loss, grieving over the death of a loved one, or just struggling with the daily-undesired vicissitudes of life. As every Nigerian woman is likely to be abused, they come to worship, abused as they are. Therefore, in good times and in bad, the Nigerian woman finds reason to identify with a faith community and usually participates more actively than their male counterpart.

---

[96] Charles Kimball, *When Religion becomes Evil* (San Francisco: HarperSanFrancisco, 2002), 33.

Pastoral Concerns

During his public ministry, Jesus in his preaching and teaching on the reign of God did not lose sight of the daily struggles and burdens of his congregation. "Come to me all you who labor and are overburdened and I will give you rest"[97] was his invitation to his congregation that constituted largely the *hoi polloi*, the oppressed of his contemporary society. He identified with the disinherited and met them at the intercession of their plights. The marginalized, oppressed women and children went to him, and he spoke to their circumstances and addressed their needs. Jesus in his transformational ministry championed the course of the emancipation of the exploited and the condemnation of the structure of sin. His first sermon, the Beatitudes, (as recorded by Luke) was about blessedness as it was about woes addressed to the oppressors of the people.[98]

What the victim of domestic violence gets from the church could be bewildering. Coming into the Nigerian church, we readily find perpetrators of domestic violence as well as their victims in the pews. Most of the time and akin to the dominant culture, the Church responds with silence, denial or disbelief of the reality of domestic violence or its effects on victims, sometimes seen as 'dirty' issue and therefore, only considered a private rather than a public matter. John McClure and Nancy Ramsey in *Telling the Truth: Preaching about Sexual and Domestic Violence*, insist that silence of church

---

[97] Mt 11:28.

[98] Lk 6: 20-26.

leaders in such sensitive and sinful issue as domestic violence is suspicious and communicates a malicious and insidious message.

> The silence, however, is not really silent. It sends a clear "hands-off" message to victims, perpetrators, and bystanders. At the very best, this silence communicates to victims that they are alone with their suffering. To perpetrators it says that the church does not hold them accountable for their evil actions. To bystanders it says that it is okay to remain on the sidelines of a brutal and sometimes deadly game."[99]

The victim of domestic violence in Nigeria is certainly, though unfortunately, alone in her suffering and alienation; the church, that is supposed to be the last beacon of hope for the oppressed offers little or no help.

Seldom therefore, is the issue of domestic violence preached about or mentioned from the pulpit. The neglect of or silence over such crucial and existential matter, especially when the liturgy suggests it, constitutes some emotional and spiritual harm to the spirit and soul of victims. It raises concern about their place in the church community and for some about their relationship with God. They feel alienated from self and from God. "There seems to be no pity sitting in the clouds that sees into the bottom of [their] grief,"[100] to use the words of William Shakespeare. Ose Aihie shares the concern

---

[99] John McClure and Nancy Ramsay, ed., *Telling the Truth, Preaching about Sexual and Domestic Violence* (Cleveland, OH: United Church Press, 1998), 2.

[100] William Shakespeare, *Romeo and Juliet,* act 3, scene 5.

that instead of being a condemnation of the perpetrators of such crime as intimate partner violence, the culture of silence reinforces the stigma victims have to bear.[101]

When therefore, the minister talks about domestic violence from the pulpit, the default is for him to instruct women on obedience to their husbands, forgiveness, redemptive suffering and the unity of marriage. It appears that while the man's role is to scatter, it is always and the duty of the woman to save marriage and maintain its unity. While the male partner seems to have no other way but battery to express his anger and aggression, the woman's lot is to ensure that her patience has no elastic limit. The man could wrong his partner as often as possible and it suffices that she forgives 'seventy times seven.' Indeed, many clergy persons exhort their female congregants always to forgive their abuser partners even before it is appropriate to do so. Such preaching can only reinforce the guilt and shame of the Nigerian woman, and bolster the arrogance and aggression of her abusive partner.

While it may be good to safeguard the unity of marriage, it is only unfair to do so via an injustice to a party. Protecting marriage, a sacred institution, while violating the divine fundamental rights of persons (victims) is robbing Peter to pay Paul. The hypocrisy of such standard unfortunately is unseen by most people in ecclesial leadership. The Roman Catholic Church emphasizes the stability of family, and describes it as the "domestic church." In *Familiaris Consortio*, Pope John Paul II described marriage and the family as one of

---

[101] Aihie, "Prevalence of Domestic Violence in Nigeria," 2-3.

the most precious of human values and acknowledged that it is under a threat by certain unjust situations that militate against its fundamental rights.[102] While the Roman Pontiff was referring to the use of contraceptives in the document, we have in domestic violence a real threat rampaging and devouring the sacred values of family and marriage. The fundamental rights of the individual members of the family or spouses is prior to the rights of the institution. A neglect of the dignity and humanity of any member of the family or union touches the foundation on which the structure stands – love. Domestic violence is a structural evil, which unsettles the love, peace and the affability of marriage and family. "Evil is something that defrauds us of some aspect of the goodness appropriate to the kind of being we are. [Domestic] Violence does this in the most obvious way. At one extreme, it deprives someone of life itself."[103] It impugns the rights and agency of women and children in the family. Arguably, marriage and family suffer more due to the perpetration of domestic violence. The values of marriage and family will be better preserved by preserving the dignity and rights of the persons that constitute the institutions.

In the end, the perpetrators, who are also in the pews, feel no remorse for the evil; they are rather empowered to forge ahead with the abuse culture. At home, the abuser male partner also taunts the

---

[102] John Paul II, *Familiaris Consortio*, (Vatican City: Vatican Press, 1981), no.1.

[103] Wendy Farley, "Evil, Violence, and the Practice of Theodicy," in *Telling the Truth: Preaching about Sexual and Domestic Violence,* ed. John McClure and Nancy Ramsay (Cleveland, OH: United Church Press, 1998), 12.

female victim with same preaching and Scripture, which he references to his advantage. The preaching fails to acknowledge the evil, condemn it or hold perpetrators accountable. Abusers seem not to be aware of the pain and suffering of victims nor are they mindful that their actions deprive others of the goodness that is at the core of their being. The emphasis on forgiveness makes it a cheap grace; it spurns the reality that forgiveness from those sinned against requires repentance, confession and accountability from the abusers. The caveat of Kroeger and Nason-Clark is worthy of note, however. "Although the Bible does exhort us to forgive, it does not insist on our returning to the circumstances that occasioned an offense in the first place. Forgiveness does not necessarily imply reconciliation. In the case of domestic violence, to continue on as before may throw open the door to continued abuse."[104] The pastor tends not to remember that to treat all humans with dignity and love is a matter of justice and right.

Sometimes, the Nigerian woman musters the courage to consult her pastor to share the burden of her abusive relationship. In the dominant culture of secrecy, the victim finds confidence in approaching her religious and spiritual leader to pour out the burden of her sorrow with the hope of being, at least, provided emotional and spiritual support. A survey in a state in southeast Nigeria reveals that most victims of domestic violence are not willing to report the

---

[104] Kroeger and Nagon-Clark, *No Place for Abuse*, 147.

incident to law enforcement agencies, but do discuss it with signifi-cant persons in their lives, including the clergy.[105] Recourse to reli-gious leaders is no surprise because of significance of religion in their lives, the spiritual authority of the clergy and the confidence that congregants repose in them. The responses of the pastors to their abused parishioners, unfortunately, are predictable when pre-sented with reports of abuse. Even on the one-on- one basis where the victim tells her personal story, there is usually a cold and insen-sitive attitude to her narrative.

Research on Church leaders that cuts across various cultural contexts in the US (Latino, Black and White populations) show that religious leaders who lack the training to respond to domestic vio-lence give counsel that is risky and can lead to deleterious outcomes. Their responses to familial abuse range from telling the victims (women) of their duty to save their spouses, to endure and be sub-missive, to asking them to forgive their abusers.[106] Some clergy em-ploy unhelpful and even dangerous approaches such as couple coun-seling, praying with the victim, asking her to read or pray certain passages of the bible or confronting the abuser.[107] The above sce-

---

[105] Okemgbo, Omidcyi, and Odimegwu, "Prevalence, Patterns and Correlates of Domestic Violence," 104.

[106] Tracia, Bent-Goodley, Noelle St. Vil, and Paulette Hubbert, "A Spirit Broken: The Black Churches Evolving Response to Domestic Vio-lence," *Social Work and Christianity* 39, no. 1 (2012): 55.

[107] Andrew Behnke, Natalie Ames, and Tina Hancock, "What Would They Do? Latino Church Leaders and Domestic Violence," *Journal of In-terpersonal Violence* 27, no.7 (2012): 1270.

nario mirrors responses of the religious leaders in the Nigerian context. The Nigerian context is such that the woman is usually to blame for any non-working relationship and family, and she is required to fix it.

An important element we want to highlight from the above-mentioned researches is the lack of training of clergy on issues of domestic violence. Most Nigerian clergy are not prepared to respond to the phenomenon. This is largely because, regrettably, it does not form part of the seminary curriculum for the training of candidates for the priesthood. During my seminary formation (1994 -2003) in one of the seminaries in the country, the phenomenon of domestic violence was not included in the curriculum. The situation has remained same until date.[108] Unequipped, the innocent priest is overwhelmed by the pastoral challenges that familial abuse poses to him. One can only expect, at best, an inadequate response or, at worst, inaction from priests who are not equipped to offer such sensitive pastoral care. They cannot offer what they have not (*Nemo dat quod non habet*). Because the Nigerian Church is yet to consider domestic violence as a pastoral issue, the pastoral/administrative tasks of diocesan/parish pastoral councils do not reflect the phenomenon either. There is no committee constituted to address it.

---

[108] For the purpose of this work I searched through the websites of all the catholic seminaries in Nigeria the result confirmed my assumption. Some do not have websites and most of them only have scanty information on their web page. I equally put a call to a couple of the academic staff of my alma mater, which further confirmed my assumption. We shall discuss this desideratum in detail in chapter eleven.

As a priest who has ministered for more than a decade in this setting, I struggled to provide support to abused parishioners. I had the goodwill and a few resources but perhaps not the required pastoral skills and resources for coping and healing. I also had the privilege of victims of marital violence tell me the reaction and attitude of their pastors to their stories of domestic abuse. The victims' reports confirm the aforementioned research findings. So, while some victims of domestic violence in Nigeria are willing to and do report cases of abuse to their spiritual leaders, the clergy response to them demonstrates at best an ignorance of the phenomenon and at worst complacence with the patriarchal socio-cultural context that sees domestic violence as "normal." Such attitude bespeaks the value we put on our women parishioners. Expressing her disappointment on the church's response to women matters, Mercy Amba Oduyoye, a Ghanaian-born and Nigerian-married woman writes: "I believe that the experience of women in the church in Africa contradicts the Christian claim to promote the worth (equal value) of every person. Rather, it shows how Christianity reinforces the cultural conditioning of compliance and submission and leads to the depersonalization of women."[109]

The above submission of Oduyoye reminds me of my experience with a catechist I worked with in a parish in Nigeria. Taking stock on coming in as pastor of the suburb parish, I inquired about marriage instructions program of the parish. The enthusiastic catechist who has served as a marriage instructor for more than a dozen years

---

[109] Mercy Amba Oduyoye, *Daughters of Anowa: African Women and Patriarchy* (Maryknoll, NY: Orbis Books, 1995), 9.

presented me with a curriculum he drafted for pre-marriage course at my request. A large part of the 8-page document contained the teaching of the Catholic Church on marriage, which are sound and healthy for the sacrament and family life. It explains marriage, its properties and ends. It also highlights the duties and responsibilities of spouses toward one another. Among the duties of women however, he wrote that the woman "**must satisfy her husband sexually** 1Cor 7: 1-5; 1Tim 2: 9-10; Prov 5: 16-23; Gen 1:28."[110] I started imagining in my mind what harm this certified catechist has done to spouses, families, church and society for these years. I was sure he is not alone in this kind of teaching. His colleagues (and perhaps some clergy) in many other parishes may be doing and teaching same. In this and sundry other ways, Christianity reinforces the cultural conditioning of subservience of women to men's whims and caprices as observed by Oduyoye. According to the catechist, some of the priests he worked with left him with the whole responsibility of instructing and preparing candidates for marriage. When I began to tell him how dangerous and unchristian the aforementioned aspect of his teaching is, his gut was to defend it based on the status quo. It took a considerable time with practical and concrete examples (some form of *conscientization*, to use Freire's term) to make him see things from a different lens and began to change his mindset.

It is equally appalling that the few of church or theological responses to the place of women in the church and society are wittingly and unwittingly massaging the culture of depersonalization of women. In a recent publication edited by Henry Opara, a Nigerian

---

[110] Emphasis is mine.

priest, titled *Pastoral Care of Women,* one unfortunately smells the primitive theology of women subjugation. While the book contains many articles that are educative and emancipatory of women, some make one querry how the publication could rightly be called a pastoral care of women. For instance, Akakuru Kingsley Ogbonnaya in his article "Women and human Sexuality" said the following about his concept of a good Christian woman, which is akin to the above-cited catechist's teaching. "A good Christian wife's focus is to make herself completely available and pleasing to her husband in order to ensure his faithfulness."[111] What Ogbonnaya is telling married women is "if your husband is unfaithful, you are responsible. It is in men's nature to be unfaithful and it is always women's marital bound-duty to forestall it for their (women's) good." This is all in the name of the Church and for the sustenance of the institution of marriage and family life.

The Church supposedly, represents a beacon of hope and the defender of marginalized and oppressed members and of society. The Catholic Church preaches and teaches about the inviolable rights of humans and our common son-ship and daughter-ship as God's cherished children. John Paul II in his Post-Synodal Apostolic Exhortation on the Vocation and Mission of the Lay Faithful in the Church and in the World - *Christifidelis Laici* - opines that the task of rediscovering as well as helping others rediscover the inviolable dignity of the human person, especially of women and children, is

---

[111] Akakuru kingsley Ogbonnaya, "Women and Human Sexuality," in *Pastoral Care of Women: In the Light of "Dignity & Vocation of Women" (Mulieris Dignitatem) of John Paul II*, Henry N. Opara ed. (Lagos, Nigeria:Marco Concepts, 2021), 66-7.

an urgent and necessary duty that the church is called to render to the human family.[112] Indeed, there is no place or time that the urgency of this call is felt as in contemporary Nigerian society. The Church in Nigeria can make further significant impact in her evangelizing mission if she would be able to consider domestic violence as a part of her ecclesial and pastoral mandate. The continued inaction and inappropriate response of clergy to victims of domestic violence affects the victims negatively as much as it raises concern about the church's support for her afflicted members. It gives a picture of a Church that cares less about the flourishing of her members. The position of religious leadership calls for responsibility in cases of abuse and challenges leadership against turning a blind eye to it or perpetuating it themselves.

Church leadership has done very little to address the suffering and pain of victims of familial violence. We contend that in a situation as in the Nigerian context where the socio-cultural factors have no resources for abused persons, the church can be a strong support system to them. It is our hope that the ongoing general church program on Synodality, which will culminate in the Bishops' Synod with the pontiff in October 2023[113] would precipitate the Nigerian

---

[112] John Paul II, *Christifidelis Laici*, (Vatican City: Vatican Press, 1988), no.18.

[113] The program of the synod on synodality provided a space where individual catholic Christians gathered in their local communities to express their concerns and ask questions on how best the church function. These questions and concerns are at the end, collected and sent to the Vatican and hoped to form the outcome of the Synod in October 2023.

Church's concerted response to domestic violence in her missionary and pastoral outreach.

It is worthwhile as we come to the end of this section to acknowledge the committed efforts of individual women and groups of women who have given their fellow women hope in the face of state and church failure. Some gallant Nigerian women from colonial era to the present time have engaged in struggles against bad socio-political and economic situations in the country and as well advocated for transformation of gender relations. From the Aba Women War (1929), the advocacy of Olufunmilayo Ransome Kuti (d. 1978), and the establishment of Women in Nigeria (1982) to the present women activists, a bunch of women have advocated and continue to advocate for representation and visibility of women in socio-political life and for general welfare of Nigerian women. These individuals and associations challenge violence against women, gender inequality and marginalization of women through socio-ideological struggles, and intellectual engagements including promoting gender studies.[114] We believe that their voices will sound louder, and perhaps yield more fruits, if more of their folks are able to join voices with them.

---

[114] Sara Panata, "It Is Not Breasts or Vaginas that Women Use to Wash Dishes: Gender, Class, and Neocolonialism through the Women in Nigeria Movement (1982-1992)," *Journal of International Women's Studies* 23, no. 2 (February 2022): 88.

SECTION II

VISION

CHAPTER SIX

THE HUMAN DIGNITY AND RIGHTS
OF VICTIMS OF DOMESTIC VIOLENCE

You Have the Body

In the history of human society, despotic and tyrannical leaders have often used incarceration as a way of wiping out the memory, power, and influence of their political opponents. Murder seems to raise great suspicion about the evil intent or action of the authority figure against his subject(s) and sometimes, it causes chaos; and so, locking the perceived enemy forever behind bars was considered a more tactical and diplomatic way of handling some political problems. However, in societies governed by laws, one of the purposes of law was to protect the citizens from such unhallowed and inglorious treatment to human bodies, hence the idea of *habeas corpus*. Habeas Corpus is a Latin expression, famous in legal vocabulary, which literarily means, "You have the body." The argument is that no human person is to face incarceration without justification by those in authority. In court therefore, the following order may be issued to the civil authority: 'Okay, you have the body of so-and-so in custody. Bring him physically in court and make your case.' The opening words of this order: habeas corpus - you have the body - were indeed dramatic in the old courts.[115] At this instance, the prisoner is presented before the court and the scene is greeted with ovational reactions.

The legal phrase: 'you have the body' is a striking and powerful way of acknowledging the importance of the human body. The idea of *habeas corpus* challenges the authority of the powerful over the bodies of others, and thus, it questions the rights of those in power over the lives of their subjects. Ill-treatment of human beings by others in society violates individuals' freedom, dignity and rights. Thomas Long and Thomas Lynch point out four implications of the legal dictum for the human person and society namely, "that human bodies matter, that selves and bodies are inextricably joined, that authorities do not have unlimited rights regarding people's bodies, and that society is just only when bodies are treated justly."[116] The first alludes to the dignity and rights of the body; the second concerns the relationship between the body and spirit; the third and the fourth point to the authority of those in leadership over their subjects and the impact their violent actions against their fellow humans has on society. We shall consider these implications in the light of our discussion on the prevalence of domestic violence in the Nigerian context. What are the implications for the Nigerian church and society? Who has the bodies of abused persons in the Nigerian society and how can these bodies be brought forth for adjudication?

---

[115] Thomas Long and Thomas Lynch, *The Good Funeral: Death, Grief, and the Community of Care* (Louisville, KY: John Knox Press, 2013), 83-84.

[116] Long and Lynch, *The Good Funeral,* 84.

Body and Soul Relationship

When Long and Lynch talk about 'selves and bodies,' they are referring to the spiritual and corporeal dimensions of the human person. According to them, "selves and bodies are inextricably joined." Consequently, what is done to the body impacts the soul and vice versa. We recognize that discourse about the relationship between body and spirit or soul, or what essentially characterizes the human person has been a major debate in the history of philosophy. Early philosophical and theological thought described humans more in terms of the spiritual. "The history of viewing the body as a disposable and not entirely worthy package for spirit — a history that extends at least from Plato, through forms of Gnosticism, to Descartes — is a long one."[117] We also find this dualism in the theological anthropology of some of the Church Fathers. These Church Fathers defended a Christian Platonism of substance dualism that conceived the body and soul as fundamentally two different substances with dissimilar attributes. According to this tradition, which has a long history of support in Christian theology, rather than the body, the personhood of the human person is grounded primarily in the soul since the soul can exist in an intermediate state as a disembodied entity.[118] The Church Fathers' emphasis was on the union of the

---

[117] Johnson, *The Revelatory Body*, 65.

[118] Marc Cortez and Michael Jensen, "Human Ontology," in *T&T Clark Reader in Theological Anthropology*, ed. Marc Cortez and Michael Jensen (New York: Bloomsbury T&T Clark, 2018), 129.

soul with God who is spirit. Patout Burns, a prominent patristic scholar writes thus:

> Christian Platonism identifies the divine image in humanity not as the autonomy of self-determination but as rationality, the human capacity for knowledge of God. It finds a connaturality between the human spirit and the divine spirit which manifests itself in a desire for union with God in knowledge and love, an innate and inalienable drive for the human toward the divine."[119]

This made them to elevate the soul over the body. Some Christian authors suggest that the dualism of the patristics was so extreme that it undermined any real appreciation of the value of the body, leading to extreme forms of asceticism and overly spiritualized understanding of the Christian life.[120] The implication is dire: a negative image of the body, however, has the tendency of casting shadows over God and his creation; God declared creation 'good' at the end of his creative activity.

With Enlightenment, however, history witnessed a decline in the regard for the spirit on the one hand, and on the other hand, an extolment of systemic materialism or what Johnson Luke Timothy

---

[119] J. Patout Burns, "Theological Anthropology," in *T&T Clark Reader in Theological Anthropology*, ed. Marc Cortez and Michael Jensen, (New York: Bloomsbury T&T Clark, 2018), 29.

[120] Cortez and Jensen, "Human Ontology," 129-130.

calls "secularization of consciousness."[121] The secularization of consciousness, according to him, refers to a certain thoroughgoing materialism that not only appreciates the empirical, but also considers the realm of the empirical to be exclusively real. In contrast to those ancients who considered spirit more real and true and worthier than matter, the modern secularist reduces everything to the material. Spirit is an unnecessary, and therefore an imaginary category. Only perceptible or sensory things are real. All material processes are aspects of a self- contained and interlocking system of material causes and effects. Science, which engages precisely such material causes and effects, replaces religion as the privileged interpreter of the world thus construed.[122]

The point at issue is that emphasis on the superiority of the soul has implications for attitude or approach to the body as much as materialism has dire consequences for the spiritual. A distortion of the unity of body and soul has often led to denigration of the body or of the soul. The understanding that the separation of the body from the self is unthinkable is evident in the habeas corpus. To hold a person's body in prison, for instance, is to have the whole person confined. One locked up in jail may have imaginations, engage in creative thinking and work but this does not make their spirit free. The prisoner's privilege to communicate with the world outside the four walls of the cell does not amount to their freedom. If a person's

---

[121] Johnson, *The Revelatory Body*, 71.

[122] Johnson, *The Revelatory Body*, 71.

body is in prison, the person is in prison. In corollary, when someone's body is abused physically or sexually, exploited emotionally or economically, the person is abused. This is because, "Our bodies make present our entire person."[123] In the words of Stephanie Paulsell, "what is essential about human being cannot be separated from our bodies...we are bodies in a very fundamental way."[124]

It follows therefore that a Church that wants to address how human lives are valued must take embodiment seriously. Persons' lived experiences take place in the body, including experience of abuse. Irenaeus, one of the church fathers, rightly observed that: "The body has to do with lived experience, so we cannot coherently think about human experience if we do not take embodiment seriously...lived, historical experiences are central to human identity."[125] The bodies of the victims of domestic violence take the scores of the suffering, pain and injustice done to them. They live with it; it weighs heavily on their soul. It is in the same bodies of ours that God encounters us. "We are inextricably implicated in our bodies and cannot distance ourselves from the body without self-distortion...Human

---

[123] Anthony Percy, *Theology of the Body Made Simple: An Introduction to John Paul's 'Gospel of the Body'* (Leominster, UK: Gracewing Publishing, 2005), 49.

[124] Stephanie Paulsell, *Honoring the Body: Meditations on a Christian Practice* (San Francisco: Jossey-Bass, 2002), 16.

[125] Sophie Cartwright "Soul and Body in Early Christianity: An Old and New Conundrum," in *A History of Mind and Body in Late Antiquity*, ed. Anna Marmodoro and Sophie Cartwright (Cambridge, UK: Cambridge Press, 2018), 177.

bodies are part of the image of God and are the means through which absolutely everything we can learn about God must come to us."[126]

A Church that values the bodies of her members as much as it does their spiritual wellbeing would help to lighten the burden of these vulnerable children of God. We must admit that Christianity's emphasis on the heavenly city and its rewards to the neglect of temporal and bodily needs often undermined the care for genuine human development and emancipation of human bodies. It is only recently that the church is beginning to affirm our common vocation to care for the temporal order. Echoing the words of the Second Vatican Fathers[127], Pope Francis acknowledges that "[i]t is no longer possible to claim that religion should be restricted to the private sphere and that it exists only to prepare souls for heaven."[128]

We look forward to the Nigerian Church that sees the divine image and likeness of human person in their body as much as in their soul. Such understanding and Christian anthropology must be reflected in the liturgy, preaching and the pastoral life of the church.

---

[126] Johnson, *The Revelatory Body*, 28-29.

[127] Second Vatican Council, "Pastoral Constitution on the Church in the Modern World, *Gaudium et Spes*, 7 December, 1965," in *Vatican Council II: The Conciliar and Postconciliar Documents,* ed. Austin Flannery (New York: Costello Publishing Company, 1975), no. 34 (hereafter cited as GS).

[128] Francis, *Evangelii Gaudium* (Vatican City: Libreria Editrice Vaticana, 2013), no. 182.

The faith education of the church is to recognize our common humanity and engender the care of the most vulnerable. The goal is to transform the minds of people to say enough is enough to the violation of human bodies in the name of cultural or religious beliefs and practices.

Bodily Dignity of Women and Children

Society's perception of the human body reflects in the manner bodies are treated. A society that recognizes the inherent dignity of the human body or person treats it with respect. One that places less value on it violates it. The prevalence of violence against women and children in Nigeria indicates the discrimination in the value of bodies. Patriarchy and subordination of women as well as lack of respect for the rights of children, have been normalized in the Nigerian socio-cultural context, and have created a situation wherein certain kinds of physicality are normative and others abused, sexualized and marginalized. This is against the right to bodily integrity, which is a basic right protected under the international law. The scenario is such that women and children are battered, sexually abused, raped and sometimes murdered. Unfortunately, the civil, cultural and religious authorities and institutions seem complacent with the status quo. This problem which we have described in the previous section as largely cultural, fails to recognize the equality of male and female and the inviolable dignity and rights of all humans. Violence perpetrated by men against women and children therefore, is a dishonor to the will of the Creator who, in the beginning, made humans -male and female- equal. "God created mankind in his image...male and female he created them."[129] Commenting on the equality that is evident in the above biblical passage John Paul II writes:

> The biblical text provides sufficient basis for recognizing the essential equality of man and woman from the point of view of their humanity. From the beginning, both are persons, unlike the other living beings in the world about them. The woman is another 'I' in a common humanity[130]

Relationship between men and women is therefore, seen not from the perspective of superiority of one over the other but from the point of view of complementarity: man and woman have the vocation to assist each other attain their God destined goals in mutual respect, dignity and equality. It is a relationship "based on mutuality and love."[131] From a theological point of view, respect for the dignity and equality of the human person, male or female, young or old, is rooted in humanity's connection with the Divine.

In the face of the contextual patriarchal challenge, the Nigerian Church must take the human body – children, women and men – seriously. A theology of the body that acknowledges the importance

---

[129] Gen 1:27.

[130] John Paul II, *Mulieris Dignitatem* (Vatican City: Vatican Press, 1988), no.6.

[131] United States Conference of Catholic Bishops, *When I Call for Help: A Pastoral Response to Domestic Violence against Women* (Washington, D.C, 2002), 5.

of the body irrespective of age or gender is essential. Habeas corpus recognizes that human bodies matter, that is, human bodies without discrimination, deserve honor, and not violated, ridiculed, or murdered. According to Donna Hicks, dignity is a birthright and as such, treating others with dignity, then becomes the baseline for interactions and relations.[132] It is right and proper that the Church treats members with dignity and as worthy of care and attention. The vision is of a Church that promotes equality of men and women, old and young, has regard for the dignity and rights of all persons, respects, accepts and enhances the difference between men and women; a situation of justice and impartiality. This would involve a transformational church leadership after the ministry of Jesus who defended the course of women, children, and the oppressed and the marginalized persons of society.

Through the incarnation, Jesus became one like us. The Word took flesh and dwelt among us.[133] The Johannian passage is devoid of a negative evaluation of human sexuality. Jesus is the image of the invisible God[134] and the perfect pattern of humanity. "Made in God's image and likeness at creation, human beings are called to be recreated in the image of Christ who is both the perfect image of God and the perfect pattern of humanity. An indispensable condition of

---

[132] Donna Hicks, *Dignity: Its Essential Role in Resolving Conflict* (New Haven, CT: Yale University Press, 2011), 4.

[133] Jn 1:14.

[134] Col 1: 15.

Christ's humanity is his body."[135] The ideal Church thus proclaims the divine image as reflected in the male as in the female body. For indeed, "it is clearly as a bodily creature that God declares humans in God's own image, for the distinction "male/female" is incomprehensible apart from the body."[136]

In considering the dignity of all bodies, the fact of the interconnectivity of human bodies comes to mind. Human bodies are interdependent and dependable. We need one another for good. The interconnectivity of human bodies demands for collective and mutual recognition of the rights and dignity of all including women and children. Human bodies share an intrinsic connection to others, to God, and to the crucified and risen Christ. This vertical (divine-human) and horizontal (human-human) connection insures the indwelling of the Spirit of God in the human body. "Do you not know that your body is a temple of the Holy Spirit within you, which you have from God?"[137] Paul questions.

First, the above passage underscores the significance of body for the apostle. According to Colleen Griffith: "Paul's likening the body to a temple of the Spirit reflects his strong valuation of the human body. The Spirit dwells in the full person, but it is the materiality of

---

[135] Benedict Guevin, *Christian Anthropology and Sexual Ethics* (Lanham, MD: University of America Press, 2002), 97.

[136] Johnson, *The Revelatory Body*, 54.

[137] 1 Cor 6: 19.

the person, the body that receives explicit mention from Paul. "Matter matters" for Paul."[138] The indwelling of the spirit in the body makes the human body symbolic. Accordingly, in his theology of the body, John Paul II opines that in the human person, both the visible and the invisible are knit together. Both are real and make up the human person. Therefore, "the human body is more than just matter. It is also the bearer of the invisible. This is what a symbol does: it makes present something that is invisible."[139] In the body lies humans' vulnerability, rawness, untidiness, limitedness, and finiteness; yet in all its vulnerability and feebleness, the female body, like its male counterpart, deserves the highest dignity and honor.

Secondly, scholars recognize that the 'body' as used by Paul in the above passage is both individual and communal. As God dwells in his temple, so he dwells in his people as individuals and as a community. The call to be temples of the Spirit has certain implications for the Body of Christ. "Individual bodily persons, as incarnate subjects, make up the communal Body of Christ. And in that Body of Christ, individual bodies are not dispensable parts of the whole: each is an irreplaceable creation gifted and graced by the Spirit's presence for the sake of the community."[140] The Church is called to recognize and celebrate the giftedness, spiritedness and embodiment of the

---

[138] Colleen Griffith, "The Spirit and the Nearness of God," in *The Holy Spirit: Setting the World on Fire*, ed. Richard Lennan and Nancy Pineda-Madrid (New York: Paulist Press, 2017), 7.

[139] Percy, *Theology of the Body Made Simple*, 38.

[140] Griffith, "The Spirit and the Nearness of God," 6.

vulnerable children of God. She must have to maintain a strong relationship between embodied individual selves and the ecclesial body. According to Griffith, lack of empathic regard in community life, abuses of power among other things are sins against the Spirit and the communal body of God's indwelling.[141]

From the foregoing, our goal is implicit, that is, to have a Church community that shows empathy for the vulnerable and abused members; a church that does not keep silence or encourage abuse of power; a congregation that provides healing and shelter to victims and survivors of familial violence. We are talking about a church community that demonstrates, in the words of Pope Francis, an artisanal fraternity. For it is by becoming artisans of fraternity that we as a Church can mend the threads of a world ripped by war and violence.[142] This is because the Church is able to see herself in the millions of women and children who suffer violence for the most part of their lives. In a video message marking the 8th International Day of Prayer and Awareness Against Human Trafficking, Pope Francis laments: "The violence suffered by every woman and every girl is an open wound on the body of Christ, on the body of all humanity; it is a deep wound that affects every one of us too."[143]

In a Church that becomes aware of her involvement and call to fraternity, servant leadership principles and participation model of

[141] Griffith, "The Spirit and the Nearness of God," 8.

[142] Francis, "Artisans of Fraternity in a World torn apart by Violence," in L'Osservatore Romano (January 2022), 7

[143] Francis, "Violence Suffered by Every Woman and Every Girl is an Open Wound," in L'Osservatore Romano (February 2022), 8.

ministry are the norm. In such a Church, leaders have a clear vision on how to say enough is enough to the violence directed against any members of their fold. Unfortunately, the Nigerian Church (and society) lack the culture of empathy for the abused. There is instead, the culture of shaming and victim blaming that perpetuates the hurt and protracts the healing of victims including when the powerful are perpetrators. The law protects the privileged but condemns the disinherited to their fate. It takes servant leadership and participation models to recognize the agency of all members, vouch for their welfare and dignity, and to give them the space to thrive.

Agency of Abused Persons

The recognition of dignity as the birthright of persons questions the reality of power abuse. As stated above, domestic violence is about men's control and power over women and children. The control is bodily, mental and spiritual as clear from the forms of familial abuse. The society reinforces this abuse of power in the home and in the public space by its inability to enact and enforce laws that guarantee the safety and rights of victims and survivors of abuse. In the Nigerian context, those in authority seem to have unlimited rights regarding the bodies and minds of the vulnerable of society. There is no recognition of women's agency. Agency, a key concept in Social Cognitive Theory, is "the ability to intentionally produce effects by one's actions. The concept of agency acknowledges that individuals construct their own development, create and negotiate their social relationships to various degrees depending on the context and their self-efficacy."[144] Agency is about the ability to exercise control over what happens to oneself; it is about the freedom to make choices about situations and relationships. Victims of domestic violence are unfortunately, denied this ability. The Nigerian society and their men strip women and children such basic human rights.

We also acknowledge that in ministering to church members, often the clergy have equally used their privileged power to abuse them. In various ways, they have disregarded the agency of women congregants. As teachers, mentors, employers, counselors, and as people vested with spiritual authority, some clergy have crossed sexual boundaries with parishioners. Other forms of abuse are not uncommon – physical, emotional, economic, spiritual. We therefore, envision a Church where ministers are aware of the duty to keep boundaries clear, and those who are involved in abuse are held accountable. This requires commitment to "pastoral and missionary conversion"[145] which arouses a sense of self-awareness and ensures fidelity to her vocation and mission. We have the vision of a Church that provides healing to the bodies and spirits of abused persons; a Church that cares more not for the reputation of their leader abusers but for the vulnerability of ordinary members; one that aims not to control but to collaborate with all and respects the integrity of members.

---

[144] Erin Green et al., "Personal, Proxy, and Collective Food Agency among Early Adolescents," *Appetite* 66 (June 2021): 1-2.

[145] Francis, *Evangelii Gaudium*, no. 25.

Essentially, habeas corpus affirms that the human body matters and cannot afford to be ill-treated unjustly by anyone, not even by those entrusted with human authority. On the contrary, under the law, those in leadership positions have the safety and security of their subjects as their primary responsibility. If one's body is treated unjustly, the one is only treated unjustly; injustice or harm done to a person's body is injustice or harm done to the person. As Margret Archer observes, humanity is the linchpin of our human agency.[146] If this is true, it follows that to deny persons their agency is to deny them their humanity. The Church in Nigeria, therefore, can only be faithful to its mission by taking the ecclesial function of *koinonia* seriously. It has to maintain a real "communion" after Jesus himself who maintained "a community of outreach and inclusion, of respect and empowerment, of compassion and commitment to justice, of partnership with servant leaders."[147] Ultimately, the Nigerian Church must guard herself against abuse of power, validate the humanity and agency of all as well as speak truth to the socio-cultural environment that treats bodies unfairly. This is crucial to her mission as an Evangelizing Church.

---

[146] Margret Archer, *Being Human: The Problem of Agency* (Cambridge, UK: Cambridge University Press, 2000), 17.

[147] Groome, *Will There Be Faith?*, 167.

CHAPTER SEVEN

THE CHURCH:
EVANGELIZING AND EMPOWERING MISSION

Identifying the Big Elephant in the Room

As the Gospel moves into a particular culture, there is an encounter. This encounter initiates a dialogue. The church's realistic
and pragmatic attitude to this meeting, theologically called inculturation, determines the fruitfulness of her missionary effort. The
Second Vatican Council (1962-1965) technically set the principles
for this practice, though the term became a theological term in the
1970's. Gerald Arbuckle, a theologian and cultural anthropologist,
defines inculturation as "a dialectical interaction between Christian
faith and cultures in which these cultures are challenged, affirmed
and transformed toward the reign of God, and in which Christian
faith is likewise challenged, affirmed, and enhanced by this experience."[148] The aim of inculturation, among other things, therefore, is
to encourage, foster and reinforce the richness of the given culture.
Our interest here is not the consideration of inculturation as it concerns the liturgical life of the church and people, which seems to be
have dominated the focus of the dialogue. While the liturgy is central
to the faith of believers, it is important that it resonate in the concreteness of their lives. Indeed, Second Vatican Council describes

---

[148] Gerald Arbuckle, *Culture, Inculturation, and Theologians: A Post-
modern Critique* (Collegeville, PA: Liturgical Press, 2010), 152.

the gap between orthodoxy and orthopraxis as "among the more serious errors of our age."[149]

Even from Arbuckle's definition of inculturation, it becomes
clear that the encounter between the Christian faith and local culture
goes beyond liturgical boundaries. It extends to the entire life and
experience of people in a given socio-cultural context. Therefore, the
task of inculturation is to address and confront the elements of a
culture that are not in congruence with God's purpose for humanity.
Arbuckle went on to say that inculturation consists of liberation of
human persons and cultures from every form of domination and injustice.[150] It is thus an act of political theology and focuses on a
Christology that involves the poor and the marginalized. Jesus, in
his public life and ministry, confronted Second Temple Judaism culture in a profound way in his pastoral ministry (as we shall expand
in the following section) and brought about a transformation that
valued the dignity of all humans especially the marginalized. Thus,
the Church in her mission not only has the task of affirming and
fostering a culture but also of challenging and transforming the cultural elements toward the reign of God. This understanding resonates with Pope Francis' vision of the Church's evangelizing mission. In his Apostolic Exhortation on the proclamation of the gospel
- *Evangelii Gaudium* - the Roman Pontiff reiterates the need to
purge cultures of traits that impede evangelization including domestic violence.

---

[149] GS, no. 43.

[150] Arbuckle, *Culture, Inculturation, and Theologians,* 170.

It is imperative to evangelize cultures in order to inculcate the Gospel...Each culture and social group needs purification and growth. In the case of the popular cultures of Catholic peoples, we can see deficiencies which need to be healed by the Gospel: machismo, alcoholism, domestic violence, low Mass attendance, fatalistic or superstitious notions which lead to sorcery, and the like.[151]

It is pertinent, first, to observe that the Pope's equation of low Mass attendance and superstitions with domestic violence as common challenges to evangelization downplays the gravity and horror of the phenomenon of domestic violence. We have indicated in the previous section that domestic violence is a structure of sin in which the ecclesial body is complicit. Whereas low Mass attendance is a matter that needs to be addressed by the Church in her mission of evangelizing all peoples (Mt 28: 19-20), domestic violence and machismo belong to a different category of deficiencies that require concerted ecclesial response at all levels of ecclesial and pastoral leadership.

Having said that, we acknowledge that Francis rightly identifies domestic violence as an ecclesial and theological issue that requires a pastoral leadership response. We have so far demonstrated that the phenomenon is a big elephant in the room, which the Nigerian Church and society have not adequately responded

---

[151] Francis, *Evangelii Gaudium*, no. 69.

to. The pope recognizes familial violence as a deficiency that requires healing. The question is: How can the Church in Nigeria go about healing the phenomenon of domestic violence through the Gospel? The Gospel is the good news of our Lord Jesus Christ, through which he proclaimed the news of humanity's freedom from sin and death. This good news is to be proclaimed and lived out for the liberation of cultures and peoples in all ages. Christianity was founded on this missionary mandate. According to the Second Vatican Council, the pilgrim Church is missionary by her very nature.[152] To engage the task of eradicating domestic violence, the Nigerian Church has first to recognize, name, and denounce domestic violence as a structure of social sin. As Kroeger and Nason-Clark rightly observed: "Giving violence a name and condemning it publicly is a tangible way that congregations and their leaders can respond directly to violence that occurs among women and men in their church family."[153] This implies that the Church must begin now to see abuse no longer as a normal situation but as an evil to fight against. Acknowledgment of the sinfulness of the phenomenon is therefore the beginning of the healing process for its victims. This is important if she has to take any action in the right direction.

---

[152] Second Vatican Council, "Decree on the Church's Missionary Activity, *Ad Gentes Divinitus*, 7 December, 1965," in *Vatican Council II: The Conciliar and Postconciliar Documents,* ed. Austin Flannery (New York: Costello Publishing Company, 1975), no. 2.

[153] Kroeger and Nason-Clark, *No Place for Abuse,* 101.

Secondly, the church has to identify domestic violence as an ecclesial matter that needs a theological and pastoral attention. This would imply that the task of eradicating it would reflect in the evangelizing mission of the local church through particular churches (dioceses) to the parish communities. Before proceeding to discuss the implications of domestic violence as a matter of theological and pastoral concern for Nigerian church, it may be necessary to highlight what she has been able to achieve in the Nigerian public space in her mission.

We must appreciate that the Nigerian Church has sometimes taken bold steps to bring the gospel to the public space in some difficult times in the history of the Nigerian state. In 1976, the Church established the Christian Association of Nigeria (CAN), which became a Christian voice in the national political sphere. Consisting of the Catholic Church and other mainline 'orthodox' protestant churches, the church umbrella body served to vouch for the wellbeing of the citizens especially the Christians in a country dominated by Muslim (often fundamentalist) leadership as well as religious crises. CAN played a key role in campaigning against the Structural Adjustment Programme (SAP) of the late 1980's (which was a World Bank programme that rather impoverished developing countries) and the surreptitious incorporation of Nigeria into the Organization of Islamic Conference (OIC) in 1986 by the Ibrahim Babangida military administration. They were also involved in the ecumenical struggle for the reversal of the annulment of the June 12

1993 presidential elections believed to be the fairest and freest election in the nation's history.[154] In the present buhari administration, the Catholic Bishops' Conference of Nigeria (CBSN) has been very vocal in calling the incumbent government to accountability for corruption and unpopular policies. In these, and some other ways, the Church advocated for rights of the citizenry and denounced corruption and injustice to the poor and oppressed masses.

However, the Pentecostal churches' growing influence in the religious landscape and subsequent dominance of CAN compromised the non-partisan status of the church umbrella body as it became obviously partisan. While this new Christian assertiveness was an attempt to resolve and push back the perceived dominant Islamic influence and the determination to position Christianity within the framework of a reimagined public space, it impacted the influence of Christian religious leadership as most genuine efforts from religious entities are now seen from the prism of Islam-Christian rivalry and struggle for dominance.

Concrete Evangelizing Measures

From the foregoing, there is no doubt that the Church has made efforts in the public space to confront the corrupt and oppressive social structures; however, her political theology omits something

---

[154] Olufemi Vaughan, *Religion and the Making of Nigeria* (Durham, NC: Duke University Press, 2016), 121, 127, 136.

that is at the core of the being of the people. What is missing is something that is socio-cultural and affects who they are as human persons. Apparently, some are more human than others in the Nigerian state, which bespeaks a basic anthropological crisis. Anthony Obinna, the prelate (now emeritus) of Catholic Archdiocese of Owerri, Southeast of the country, espoused a pastoral theology of *theofiliance*[155] in which he established a theological anthropology that responds to the anthropological crisis of the Nigerian society. Commenting on this crisis, which Obinna's theology of theofiliance sets out to address, Bede Ukwuije writes:

> This crisis is crystallized in the distortion in the way fellow humans perceive, react, and relate to one another. The consequence of this anthropological crisis is the growing violence to the sacredness and preciousness of the human person as well as the negation of the humanity of the other."[156]

---

[155] Theofiliation is Anthony Obinna's coinage, which explains his theological thought about humanity's relationship to God through Christ and to one another. The theofiliation dynamic considers every form of discrimination as ungodly. A compendium of this theology was published in a monograph titled "Emerging conversations on Theofiliation: Essays in honour of Archbishop Anthony J.V Obinna" in 2019.

[156] Bede Ukwuije, "Theofiliance and the Reconfiliation Dynamic: Healing Humanity's Divisions through the Memory of the Cross," in *Emerging Conversations on Theofiliation: Essays in Honour of Archbishop Anthony J.V. Obinna*, ed. Kenneth Ameke and Samuel Uzoukwu (Bloomington, IN: Xlibris, 2019), 244.

A protrusive phenomenon, which negates "the humanity of the other" and one, which is focal to Obinna's theological anthropology, is the *Osu Caste System* that is inherent in the socio-cultural belief and life of the Igbo people of Nigeria.

The Osu Caste System is an ancient practice in Igboland that discourages social interaction and marriage with a group of people, referred to as Osu (outcasts). This is because they dedicate these Osu people to the Alusis (deities) and are thus seen as inferior to the Nwadiala (free-borns)."[157]

Besides the marriage prohibition, the discrimination disallows the *Osus* from taking traditional titles in the community and from breaking the kolanut.[158] The fight for the abolishment of the *Osu Caste System* is ongoing and has recorded significant success in contemporary Igbo society. Traditional rulers, scholars, and advocacy groups have become more involved and are committed to end this social discrimination and dehumanization of men, women and children based on this idolatrous belief and practice. Obinna's voice is distinct in the campaign against the *Osu* culture that defies basic hu-

---

[157] Franklin Ugobude, "Culture: The Osu Caste System in Igboland," *The Guardian Newspaper* (Nigeria), November 18, 2018.

[158] Among the Igbo of Nigeria, Kolanut is regarded as a sacred fruit and thus is revered. Because of its sacredness and centrality in the people's culture and tradition, the osus are not allowed to present it in a public function.

man rights and stigmatizes humans created in the image of God. According to the Archbishop: "All men and women were created equal by God and in his own image. Christianity came around to abolish fetishism and all other forms of bondage and social discrimination… The [*Osu*] caste system is primitive and inhuman and must be abrogated."[159] He took the advocacy to the conference of his colleagues of the Igbo extraction. Earlier in March 2022, shortly before his retirement, the Catholic Bishops of Igboland (Onitsha and Owerri Provinces) jointly issued a Pastoral Directive to the effect of ending the Osu-Diala divide. The document titled "No More Divide into Diala/Amadi-Osu-Ume-Ohu" is meant to take the battle against the idolatrous and inhuman discrimination to the grassroots, at every strata of community and church in the Igbo society. The expectation is to bring to an end the discrimination among the Igbos especially as it concerns marriages, Ezeship, title conferment, and appointments to various offices in the community and church.[160]

The crusade against the *Osu Caste System* is commendable; kudos to the Archbishop emeritus and to all persons and groups in ecclesial and civil circles behind this development. However, unfortunately, little or no mention is made of a sister sinister practice that is equally deeply rooted in the people's culture. I argue that we can

---

[159] Daily Post Staff, "Catholic Bishop, AJV Obinna seeks end to 'Osu' Caste Systen in Igboland," *Daily Post Newspaper* (Nigeria), August 7, 2021.

[160] Catholic Bishops of Onitsha and Owerri Ecclesiastical Provinces, *No More Divide into Diala/Amadi-Osu-Ume-Ohu* (Owerri, Nigeria: Assumpta Press, 2022), 2.

make a similar progress in the area of domestic violence if ecclesial leadership responds adequately. As has been established in the previous section, familial abuse is a phenomenon that cuts across all ethnic and religious groups in Nigeria. It therefore requires the Church to get into the messiness of the culture and carry out a healing from the root (*sanatio in radice*). This is an obviously radical task which makes it imperative for religious leaders to accompany their church community members and be ready to "put some feet to their prayers"[161] after Jesus, the Good Shepherd, who defends his sheep against the wolves.

To this end, the vision is that the Catholic Bishops' Conference of Nigeria would issue an official document on domestic violence and violence against women, like their counterparts in the US[162] and in other nations of the world. Such pastoral publication would be a testimony of their commitment to the fight against this social deficiency. We must acknowledge that the Nigeria bishops in 2017 issued a document titled *Guidelines for Processing Cases of Sexual Abuse of Minors and Vulnerable Adults*. The issuance of the document may have been prompted by the litigations against the clergy

---

[161] Tran, *Reset the Heart*, 3.

[162] The Catholic bishops of the United States affirmed their stance against domestic violence and their support for victims of domestic violence in a pastoral document "*When I Call for Help: A Pastoral Response to Domestic Violence*" published in 2002. The document condemns the use of Scripture to justify violence against women. Catholic Bishops Conferences of many countries have similar documents.

in recent times in the West on abuse of minors. (It was a precaution-
ary measure knowing that some of the clergy of the local church
have become perpetrators of such abuses). At a more fundamental
level, the Nigerian ecclesial leadership are to ensure that domestic
violence forms part of the seminary curriculum for the training of
candidates for the priesthood. Priests should learn to refer victims
of abuse and perpetrators to appropriate forms of counseling when
necessary. Indeed, the clergy who vowed to care for the flock of God
entrusted to their care ought to come to the full awareness that the
dignity of each person, including the least of the brethren, is the first
act of care. Together as a Church, we can ensure the growth of an
economy of care that makes for a healthy Church.[163]

At the diocesan and parish levels, I envision pastoral/adminis-
trative mandate of the pastoral councils to enshrine domestic violence in their agenda and/or have a committee constituted to address it. The collaboration of the pastoral team members is crucial
to addressing such adaptive leadership issue, which is not just a technical problem that is easily fixable. Recognizing that the teaching
ministry is primary task of the clergy,[164] preaching against the phenomenon and other forms of faith education becomes inevitable for
a Church that takes her evangelizing mission seriously. Pope Francis

---

[163] Pope Francis, "Violence Suffered by Every Woman and Every Girl
is an Open Wound," in *L'Osservatore Romano* (February 2022), 8.

[164] Second Vatican Council, "Decree on the Ministry and Life of
Priests, *Presbyterorum Ordinis*, 7 December, 1965," in *Vatican Council II:
The Conciliar and Postconciliar Documents*, ed. Austin Flannery (New
York: Costello Publishing Company, 1975), no. 4.

appreciates the fact that the task of confronting and transforming cultural deficiencies is not an easy one, realizing how difficult the task of transforming a dominant culture is. Yet, the church as an evangelizing community, aiming to touch "the suffering flesh of Christ in others" has to be "supportive, standing by people at every step of the way, no matter how difficult or lengthy this may prove to be."[165]

We envision a Church that fosters a theological anthropology that upholds the essential goodness of all humans after the Creator, God; a community of faith that considers the human flourishing of its members a part of ecclesial and pastoral mission. The task of the Church that holds such a Christian anthropology is obvious: "to care for human well-being, physical and spiritual, personal and social."[166] Indeed, a Church that neglects the physical, emotional and psychological needs of her members is simply miles away from the example of Jesus. As Michael Washington observes: "It is important to view the ministry of Jesus and that of his disciples as ministry of care for the physical, emotional, and mental needs of persons. Without that recognition, Jesus's ministry takes on an exclusively spiritual form, where spiritual connotes a kind of disembodied existence."[167] A Church that recognizes and promotes the all-embracing and multi-

---

[165] Francis, *Evangelii Gaudium*, no. 24.

[166] Groome, *Will There Be Faith?*, 185.

[167] Michael Washington, "Care with Persons both Healthy and Unhealthy," in *Covenant Quarterly* 76, nos 3-4, (August-November 2018): 44, http://www.covquarterly.com

dimensional ministry of Jesus is on the trajectory of becoming an empowering Church.

The Empowering Mission of the Church

This book strongly condemns domestic violence and advocates for its total eradication. We are aware of the millions of vulnerable Nigerians who are experiencing suffering, pain and hurt because of various kinds of abuse from people who though avowed to love them. We do not presume to see an end to familial violence even by means of this piece of work. We rather hope to raise awareness of the heinousness of the dehumanization, insist that it is something not fashionable in our time and age, and ultimately take some con- crete transformational steps to change the stories of victims and sur- vivors of domestic violence in Nigeria. The question is: What do we owe the abused persons of our population? Put in another way: In a society bedeviled with so many socio-political and economic up- heavals, how can the faith community offer hope to her members and others who are victims and survivors of familial violence? In our time and age, the Church in Nigeria cannot afford to respond with silence, indifference or denial to the suffering of a significant num- ber of her members often with perpetrators and victims in the church pews. Indifference and denial keep us locked in our comfort zone and consequently prevent genuine effort to initiate changes into the system. Domestic violence can no longer remain a private matter if the Church clearly understands and appreciates her salvific mission.

As we explained in chapter one, the history of human society witnessed a seeming justification of domestic violence within the religious framework and Christianity in particular legitimized violence against women and children with roots from the Greco-Roman culture and proof from the bible.[168] The Western Christianity transported and reproduced in their mission territories in Africa including Nigeria this teaching and practice of male dominance. Western Christianity at its origins in Nigeria, therefore, met a culture similar in nature in terms of the perception of women and children as subordinates who have the menfolk violate their rights. The combination of a culture and a religion that perpetuate abuse of women and children has worked against the flourishing of victims and survivors in the Nigerian society.

With modernity, however, societies are reawaking to the atrocities of the traditional hierarchical understanding of gender and generational relations that made women men's subordinates. Modern civilizations are fast in eliminating the unjust social structures that impugn the dignity of women. The Second Vatican Council with its *aggiornamento*[169] spirit illustrated the Church's opening to the modern world. In its pastoral constitution on the Church in the Modern

---

[168] Timmers-Huigens, "Christian Faith and Justification of Domestic Violence," 169.

[169] Aggiornamento is an Italian phrase, which means bringing up to date; it depicts the wave of renewal and reform, which the church was ready to embrace as it inaugurated the Second Vatican Council in 1962 in the face of the challenge of modernity.

World, the council fathers condemned various forms of discrimination and dehumanization as being against the will of God for humanity. "With respect to the fundamental rights of the person, every type of discrimination, whether social or cultural, whether based on sex, race, color, social condition, language or religion, is to be overcome and eradicated as contrary to God's intent."[170] Nevertheless, for more than half a century after the Council, the Church has been struggling with living out the principles of the epochal assembly. Indeed, the official declarations of the Church seem far removed from the lived reality in the church.

In the spirit of the Council, however, and in response to the challenges of the US modern Church, the US Conference of Catholic Bishops (USCCB) in 1992 issued a pastoral letter to condemn domestic violence and the use of Scripture to justify violence against women. The document, revised in 2002 in part, reads:

As bishops, we condemn the use of the Bible to support abusive behavior in any form. A correct reading of Scripture leads people to an understanding of the equal dignity of men and women and to relationships based on mutuality and love. Beginning with Genesis, Scripture teaches that women and men are created in God's image. Jesus himself always respected the human dignity of women.[171]

---

[170] GS, no. 29.

[171] United States Conference of Catholic Bishops, *When I Call for Help*, 5.

Silence, indifference, and the use of Scripture to justify the phenomenon by the Nigerian Church spells disaster to the church and society; it shows, at best, the Church as complacent with the patriarchal socio-cultural context that sees domestic violence as "normal." The words of the US bishops are empowering to victims of violence and that is what the Nigerian women need to hear from their church leaders.

Victims and survivors are in need of healing and empowerment within the Church. Trauma is as one of the effects of domestic violence. Victims make tremendous efforts to cope with their everyday lives. Studies in trauma and spirituality indicate that spirituality plays a major role in resilience for trauma survivors. In their research to find out the extent to which victims of sexual assault record a changed role for spirituality in their lives and the degree to which this tendency is related to change in individual well-being or recovery, James Kennedy, Robert Davis and Bruce Taylor, observed that faith could enhance a person's ability to cope with negative life event. The research indicated that 60% of the victims (of sexual abuse) reported an increased role of spirituality and appeared to have restored well-being in their 9-24 months after a sexual assault.[172] Change in spirituality therefore, correlates with change in well-being. This suggests that religious changes merit consideration

---

[172] James Kennedy, Robert Davis, and Bruce Taylor, "Changes in Spirituality and Well-Being among Victims of Assault," *Journal for the Scientific Study of Religion* 37, no.2 (June 1998): 325.

in faith practice and coping. Dawnovise Fowler and Michele Rountree's research on "Exploring the Meaning and Role of Spirituality for Women Survivors of Intimate Partner Abuse" concluded that both spirituality and religion promote recovery by offering hope and forestalling feelings of helplessness, while allowing survivors to give meaning and purpose to life-events and suffering.[173]

It is not a surprise that many abused persons turn to religious communities for support, solace, and the hope of finding a safe place.[174] Lehner-Hartmann observes that since social institutions (especially churches) have high moral authority, victims of domestic violence look to them as a resource for how they are to assess their experiences before other humans and before God.[175] In Nigeria, church leaders are a force to be reckoned with. Their position of moral authority is considerable and recognized. Since victims turn to the church, the church and her leaders ought to foster the wholeness and emancipation of these needy members of the community. Our expectation is that the Church in Nigeria becomes an empowering Church. A crucial way by which the Nigerian Catholic Church

---

[173] Dawnovise N. Fowler and Michele A. Rountree, "Exploring the Meaning and Role of Spirituality for Women Survivors of Intimate Partner Abuse," *The Journal of Pastoral Care and Counseling* 63, no.3 (September 2009): 78.

[174] Denise Starkey, "The Roman Catholic Church and Violence against Women," in *Religion and Men's Violence against Women*, ed. Andy Johnson (New York: Springer, 2016), 190.

[175] Lehner-Hartmann, "Familial Violence against Women as a Challenge for Theology and Ethics," 122.

can address the issue of domestic violence is by a compassionate support to its victims and survivors who look up to her in such moments of pain and suffering. It becomes necessary to ask the following important questions: what images of marriage and family do the Church hold? What would victims and survivors of domestic violence hear about abuse, sin, forgiveness and reconciliation in a Church they are bona fide members?

Doctrine and Life

In marriage and family, love, trust, fidelity, and security are significant features. Traditional catholic theology stresses that wives are to be submissive to their husbands and men are to love their wives and this teaching unfortunately has no checks and measures against domination and subordination relations between man and woman, and between parents and children that result from the relationships. Emphasis and an appreciation of the equal humanity of men and women, which recognizes the mutuality and love in marriage and family is important. Empowerment, therefore, would consist in orienting women to realize that the price for love cannot be violence; violence rather destroys love, trust, fidelity and security, and hence destroys marriage. Abusive husbands in turn are required to be oriented to be aware that violence is not a legitimate means to attain their aims or desires. They need to know that their behavior contradicts the purpose of marriage and its author's will for humanity. More theologically, abusive spouses receive the teaching that makes them know that their behavior is sinful and that they are accountable for it. The Nigerian Church has to be ready to hear the woman's story and recognize her agency about her marriage. This means that she must not be persuaded to remain in an abusive relationship.

In preaching and teaching about domestic violence, the clergy often advice victims to see their suffering as redemptive, akin to the suffering of Christ. This is cruel and can forestall healing. It is, therefore, necessary to make a distinction between Christ's suffering for the redemption of humankind and the suffering of a woman in an abusive relationship. Christ, on the one hand, voluntarily accepted suffering that wrought our redemption; he permitted sin in order to do away with it at a profound level. He made the choice to fulfill the ultimate goal of redeeming humanity. On the other hand, the victim of violence does not freely choose to be violated; violence is inflicted upon them against their will. Victim's suffering gives room for the continuation of the abuse by the perpetrator. Violence against a fellow human person is a crime against humanity. A culture or theology of suffering that allows humans to afflict fellow humans cannot, in any way bring salvation to the perpetrator. A woman may suffer for her faith, but brutality at the hands of her husband who unduly exercises control over her is a different thing all together. Such suffering that permits a perpetrator to continue an abusive behavior cannot be redemptive. Instead, it incurs sin, which inflicts harm to the soul of victim and perpetrator.[176]

---

[176] Kroeger and Nagon-Clark, *No Place for Abuse*, 129,132.

The above understanding of suffering is liberating to both the abused and the abuser. For the abused, it frees her from guilt feeling when she makes up her mind to assert her agency, to discontinue an abusive relationship, and to see the concept of her suffering being redemptive as a myth. Such understanding helps the perpetrator to feel accountable for his action, have a sense of guilt, and not to see redemption where it is not.

Often, victims of domestic violence are persuaded to forgive offenders and reconcile with them. In the Christian religious teaching and practice, there exists the assumption that the burden of forgiveness is the responsibility of the violated. In most ethnic groups in Nigeria also, the woman who is abused by her husband is expected ask him for forgiveness. Among the Igbos, the women often is required to seek for forgiveness by presenting the abuser with an item or gift to placate his angry. In the end, the victim is expected to experience peace and healing. This is the common expectation of family, relatives, friends, community and church. Unfortunately, by going this trajectory, women who have suffered physically and emotionally only end up feeling guilty for the abuse and believing that their behavior was responsible for their experience. Consequently, their pain and anguish are suppressed and unaddressed, and the offender continues with his abusive behavior.

However, from Jesus' theology of forgiveness, we encounter a theology that links the expectation of forgiveness by the offended to genuine confession and repentance on the part of the offender. In Luke 17:3-4, Jesus teaches that the one who sins against another should be rebuked and is forgiven if they show repentance. This teaching of Jesus, as Marie Fortune rightly observes, implies justice, which is required for real forgiveness and for true healing to take place.[177] In considering the theological concept of forgiveness, the Church in Nigeria must bring to focus the cardinal the virtue of justice. Following the principle of justice, forgiveness by victims requires the offender to take three steps namely, acceptance of guilt and responsibility for the action, repentance, and restitution. It suffices here to say that: "Repentance demands more than just remorse. Repentance in the sense of *metanoia* demands a fundamental change. And this is not accomplished through good intentions; it requires time, hard work and therapy."[178] Finally, the offender has to take a concrete action to make restoration for the harm. It is only in this scenario of justice that interpersonal forgiveness is possible. The Church in Nigeria can ensure this theology of forgiveness via preaching, catechesis, premarital instructions and through her sundry means of faith education. In fairness, the offender rather ought to be the one to come up with a gift item to pacify the harmed. It is the element of justice that brings healing and emancipation to the victim and conversion to the abusive partner. (We shall discuss the issue of responsibility in the following chapter under accountability for perpetrators).

---

[177] Marie Fortune, "Preaching Forgiveness?" in *Telling the Truth: Preaching about Sexual and Domestic Violence,* ed. John McClure and Nancy Ramsay (Cleveland, OH: United Church Press, 1998), 50.

[178] Lehner-Hartmann, "Familial Violence against Women as a Challenge for Theology and Ethics," 129.

In the end, the Church becomes a safe place for all her members, a community where victims and survivors of familial violence receive support and resources on the trajectory to human flourishing and wholeness. The Church cannot afford to contradict her teaching on compassion, mercy and sacramentality. Such teachings recognize our common humanity and agency, and our responsibility toward one another especially to the needy and afflicted. Appropriate clergy responses make the victim of domestic violence "walk tall with certainty that God loves her and that she deserves the fullness of life that God wills for all God's precious children."[179] The expectation is that domestic violence victims receive from their pastors and faith community the pastoral care and resources they deserve for empowerment and emancipation. As a Church that has encountered a culture that marginalizes a segment of people who are God's children, it behooves the Nigerian Catholic Church to be the voice of the voiceless after Jesus who always stood for the marginalized and oppressed. The challenges facing abused women in Nigeria are urgent and require the Church's active participation and genuine intervention. We must be present to them and identify with them at the intersection of their concrete and intricate life challenges.

---

[179] Cooper-White, *The Cry of Tamar*, 148.

CHAPTER EIGHT

RESTORING THE DIGNITY AND RIGHTS OF VICTIMS OF DOMESTIC VIOLENCE: FURTHER IMPLICATIONS FOR CHURCH AND STATE

Religion and society exert so much influence on individuals, constituent families and culture. This is evident in the role religious and civil institutions and leadership play in perpetuation of violence, which we were able to show in the previous chapters. Equally, any meaningful and successful program or step to mitigate this phenomenon necessarily involves Church and State. The restoration of the dignity and rights of vulnerable population of society, therefore, has several implications for religious and civil leadership. Some of these have been highlighted above, especially those that bother on religious authorities. The Nigerian church and political leadership have a duty towards ensuring the dignity and rights of the most vulnerable members of community and society. To achieve this, there must be a sane attitude to power, accountability by perpetrators of abuse, and collaboration in providing support to victims of violence by the Church and State.

Understanding Power

In the summer of 2021, Ghanaians and indeed Africans were greeted with the news of a clergyman who was freely kissing female congregants during a public worship. The shocking video, which went viral on social media, saw the Ghanaian Anglican priest excitingly kissing several female students of a College of Education in Ashanti from the pulpit. The priest, fully dressed in his full liturgical regalia, stood by the pulpit as the young women filed in a single line processed to the altar area to have the church leader give them a kiss in their mouth. The congregating students stood helplessly shouting as they watched with dismay at the sacrilegious act.[180] This is a concrete case of abuse of power, a situation that is not uncommon in Nigerian, nay, African homes, churches and societies.

Power, in its very basic sense is the power of the individual to be able. It derives from the Latin word *posse* which means "to be able" from which equally is derived potency and potential. According to Ruth Layzell, the most obvious definition of power is that it is the energy we possess that enables us to be and to act. It is the capacity to act in effective ways with things and people that form part of our world.[181] Exploring the issue of abuse in religious settings, she asserts that abuse in ecclesial contexts is simply a misuse of power. Power is something that we all have to some degree. As Michel Foucault (1926-1984), a contemporary French Philosopher, says, power is

---

[180] Cletus Ukpong, "Priest Filmed Kissing Female Students during Church Service," *Premium Times Newspaper* (Nigeria), August 17, 2021.

[181] Ruth Layzell, "Pastoral Counselling with those who have experienced abuse in religious settings," in *Clinical Counselling in Pastoral Settings*, ed. Gordon Lynch (New York: Routledge, 1999), 108-109.

everywhere and comes from everywhere, and consists in a multiplicity of force relations.[182] Authority gives a privilege of power. The history of civil and religious authority has shown that people in authority often use their privileged positions and offices to control, and sometimes to violate their subjects.

Foucault describes how power relations in the pre-enlightenment era served the Church and monarchs who had absolute sovereignty and suppressed the people with power believed to be a gift from God. He equally explained how the modern times ushered in a 'reformed system' where power functions in terms of relations between different components, institutions and other groups within the state. However, in the reformed system, power still functions, similar to the pre-enlightenment period, to dominate and mold people in order to keep them under the services and sway of the state.[183] For Foucault, whose analysis of power has been appropriated by scholars of religious studies and theology, power is something not acquired; it is contingent, "exercised from innumerable points, in the interplay of nonegalitarian and mobile relations."[184] This is to say that rather an individual holding power, instead it circulates in the system.

In some feminist circles, there is a discourse on a threefold typology of power understood as power-over, power- with and power-

---

[182] Jeremy Carrette, *Foucault and Religion: Spiritual corporality and political spirituality* (New York: Routledge, 2000), 148.

[183] Geoff Danaher, Tony Schirato and Jen Webb, *Understanding Foucault* (Thousand Oaks, CA: Sage Publications Ltd, 2000), 68-70.

[184] Danaher, Schirato, and Webb, *Understanding Foucault*, 70-71.

within. Cooper-White explains that this threefold typology gained consensus within certain feminists in the 1980s and 1990s. *Power-over* is the understanding of power as dominance over others. Power in this case is utilitarian and thus an instrument to have control over others. *Power-with* contains the element of mutuality in relationship with the other. It involves negotiation, mutual concern and respect. Implicit in the power-with is the *power-within*, that is, the power of the self, the authentic voice of the individual. The power-within refers to the potential of one's own inner wisdom, intuition and self-esteem.[185] From the feminist analysis, power-over, which unfortunately is the predominant understanding of power, is destructive to individuals, society and the planet. Power-with and power-within are power formulations intended to typify mutuality, justice, responsibility and care.[186]

The above typology shows that there is usually an abuse of power in the context of power-over. In this case, power seems immobile but is held by the powerful who exploit the vulnerability of those they supposedly care for in order to advance their stake. This is true in the case of the priest who sexually harassed the female college students during a public worship. There was no negotiation, mutuality or respect for the innocent, young women. Even though the women subtly resisted the sexual harassment, the pastor used force and intimidation to have his way. This is also true in families where the men exercise control over their spouses and in the state where the

---

[185] Cooper-White, *The Cry of Tamar*, 53-55.

[186] Cooper-White, *The Cry of Tamar*, 55.

elected political leaders exploit the masses. Jesus expressed his abhorrence of this "lording it over" model of leadership. "You know among the gentiles those they call their rulers lord it over them, and their great men make their authority felt. Among you this is not to happen."[187]

Rightly understood, power or authority is not meant to tear down people or relationships but to build up. This is the Pauline concept of power. Writing to the Corinthian church, Paul assured them that he exercises his apostolic authority, which comes from Christ, not in a manner that knocks persons and the community down but in a way that builds them up.[188] Apparent in Paul's notion of power is his emphasis on sameness, which seems to obscure differences among the community of believers. Thus, he speaks about the elimination of differences in identity and social stratifications. According to him, "there is neither Jew nor Greek, there is neither slave nor free, there is no male and female, for you are all one in Christ Jesus."[189] While some scholars argue that in Pauline discourse, the elimination of differences is principally an attempt to create egalitarian Christian communities in the early church, others opine that Paul was simply responding to a strict political opposition to form a community of single social identity and unity.

Elizabeth Castelli, a feminist theologian, in her critique of Paul's concept of power opines that the apostle was not in any way advo-

---

[187] Mk 10:42-43.

[188] Cf 2 Cor 10: 8; 13:10.

[189] Gal 3: 28.

cating the breaking down of boundaries and creating a new, egalitarian community devoid of hierarchical social arrangements.[190] Continuing, Castelli argues that Paul's idea of power within the Christian community is one in which there is power relations negotiated and struggled over in typically human social networks. Paul's goal was the institutionalization of power, the bringing about of the unity and harmonization in the early Christian communities, which are a kind of condensed analogy for the more universalization of Christian discourse. Castelli concluding by saying that the Pauline concept of power "worked" in creating part of the ground for Christian hegemony on the West.[191]

The influence of Pauline theology in general and his notion of power in particular, no doubt, has remained a strong force from early Christianity and thought up until today. A true egalitarian Christian community never existed and may not have been inferred by Paul. The thrust of this work is not a discourse on institutionalization of power. However, it suffices to say that institutionalization has its strength and weakness. Jeremy Carrette rightly observes that religion after Foucault always exists as a system of power, which orders people's lives via asset of force relations. It does so not by violently coercing people to engage in certain acts but by shaping them to carry out a particular way of life voluntarily.[192] Power has a mobilizing force and is instrumental to our ability to construct living

---

[190] Elizabeth Castelli, *Imitating Paul: A Discourse of Power* (Louisville, KY: John Knox Press, 1991), 130.

[191] Castelli, *Imitating Paul*, 131.

[192] Carrette, *Foucault and Religion*, 149.

style. It can be said that, "[t]here is no ideal or neutral pattern of living, only different forms of living set against each other – however, the ethical question remains as to which of these are more or less oppressive.[193]

Paul's understanding of pastoral power as "an authority that is for building up and not for breaking"[194] is a denouncement of power as power-over and the recognition of the agency and self-esteem of others in relationship. This understanding seems to align more to the servant leadership model spoken about by Susan Wood where leadership is seen as a privileged opportunity of person to represent a group or community, a representative leadership where headship is understood as standing in the place of the community on behalf of the community.[195] Appraising this Pauline understanding of power, Kroeger and Nason-Clark write: "Paul's essential analysis of power and authority is that it is given to build up and not to tear down; its purpose is not self-aggrandizement or to have one's own way; it is to be used in sharing rather than in dominating; it stems from service developed within a context of humility and voluntary restriction of power."[196] In this way, the exercise of power is for the good of others and thus, linked with service. The leader, in this case, becomes a servant.

---

[193] Carrette, *Foucault and Religion*, 149.

[194] 2 Cor 12: 10.

[195] Susan Wood, "The Priestly Identity: Sacrament of Ecclesial Community," *Worship* 69, no. 2 (March 1995): 115.

[196] Kroeger and Nason-Clark, *No Place for Abuse*, 159.

To ensure the dignity and rights of the most vulnerable in the community and society, the Nigerian church and state must assume the servant-leadership model. This model understands leadership as a privileged opportunity of people to serve as representatives, which according to Robert Greenleaf is organic and persuasive, and usually greeted with voluntary acceptance.[197] Servant-leaders recognize the agency of their subjects and are ready to serve them. Power in this case is inclusive and participatory, and all receive treatment that accord them dignity and respect as subjects-in-relationship. In this way, church members have a sense of belonging and safety in the house of God, and the state feels obligated to ensure the flourishing of its population. This brings us to the issue of accountability.

Accountability by Perpetrators

Every act of violence is an unjust action. Someone is hurt, dehumanized by another. The victim has their rights denied them and their dignity trampled upon. Thus, victims of domestic violence suffer moral injury. Even though some scholars argue that the concept of moral injury should be strictly used in the context of military service from where the concept originated, others have insisted that it can be applied in other concepts of human experience that reliably

---

[197] Robert Greenleaf, *The Servant Leader* (New York: Paulist Press, 1977), 24.

generate conditions that are morally injurious.[198] Following the understanding of the latter, domestic violence as a terrible and cruel human experience morally injures its victims. Moral injury involves the violation of 'what is right' by an individual who wields legitimate authority; it takes place due to a betrayal by person(s) occupying legitimate authority.[199] In the family, the man as a domestic head is an authority figure and the violation of the dignity and rights of their children and women affects their moral beliefs and expectations. In the same vein, when the church or civil (including police, legislative and justice systems) authorities fail to protect the humanity of the vulnerable or violate same, they disrupt their moral link to God and to society, which they internalized and so cause them moral wounds.

Consequently, justice becomes a necessary element in dealing with domestic violence, and accountability is part of the justice making. Writing about her experience of pastoral work with victims and survivors of domestic, Marie Fortune, Founder and Senior Analyst of the *FaithTrust Institute* (formerly The Center for the Prevention of Sexual and Domestic Violence), stated that for healing and emancipation, justice was required. Abused persons request the abuser to acknowledge what they did, render an apology or repent, be sure

---

[198] Joseph McDonald, "What is Moral Injury? Current Definitions, Perspectives and Context" in *Moral Injury: A Guidebook for Understanding and Engagement*, ed. Brad Kelle (Lanham, MD: Lexington books, 2020), 14-15.

[199] Jane Tillman, "Intergenerational Transmission of Suicide: Moral Injury and the Mysterious Object in the Work of Walker Percy," *Journal of the American Psychoanalytic Association* 64, no. 3 (June 2016): 544.

they don't abuse others, make restitution and speak to the abuser's superior in case of clergy abuse. Justice therefore, lies in telling the truth about the act, compassion, protection of the vulnerable, vindication of the victim, acknowledgement by someone significant to victim/survivor, restitution to the survivor, and accountability for the offender.[200]

The safeguard for accountability and justice are civil and ecclesial authorities. Violence would go on unabated without having perpetrators be responsible for their evil actions. Accountability can help unlearn the violence. It is by holding offenders accountable that the church and state communicate that violence is a harmful behavior that must be put to a stop. The Nigerian state could hold perpetrators accountable by enacting and enforcing laws that protect the vulnerable, allowing the truth of violence be told, providing compensation for the survivor, and bringing the offender to book. The domestication of the treaties on the elimination of violence against women and children by the Nigerian state is inevitable. In addition, they are to provide counseling and corrective opportunities to offenders, as they also require healing from their abusive inclinations. The Church is to declare their communities domestic violence-free, and make clear their commitment to fight against marital violence in all its ramifications. Preaching and teaching must concretely demonstrate this objective in a manner that is not suspicious. Finally, church leadership must be held accountable for clergy abuse.

---

[200] Marie Fortune, "Preaching Forgiveness," 54.

The report about the abuser clergyman, told at the beginning of this chapter, revealed that the school authorities were looking for the student(s) that recorded and shared the clip.[201] The action of the priest did not embarrass them; they were rather concerned only about the atrocity going public. The implication is that these bystanders saw nothing wrong with the action of the clergy person, or they were afraid to hold the perpetrator responsible for the abusive behavior or were more concerned about saving the image of the priest or the church. In any case, it bespeaks the prevalent dominant culture of abuse and accomplices to the crime. The action of the school authorities certainly undermines the harm done to the abused students and is a threat (emotional abuse) to those who reacted rightly by making the matter public. Ultimately, the situation perpetuates violence and consequently constitute a permanent denial of the dignity and rights of the vulnerable of society. The report went further to announce that the metropolitan archbishop of the local church did respond in an official statement expressing the sadness and embarrassment that the action of the priest had brought to the church stating that investigations had already commenced into the matter, which they would deal with in accordance with the church's norms and values.[202] This is a step in the right direction in terms of accountability. The troubling question however, is whether the church will solely be responsible for investigation and execution

---

[201] Ukpong, "Priest Filmed Kissing Female Students during Church Service."

[202] Ukpong, "Priest Filmed Kissing Female Students during Church Service."

of justice in this matter. One wonders what sort of justice the church body will able to provide to address adequately the abuse without the state laws and justice system. The church in this case becomes a judge in her case. Again, though they offered to provide counseling services to the affected students, it is not certain how far and effective they may go with it.

The picture we have before us in this abuse situation is that the public abuse is simply and purely a church matter to be handled by the ecclesial body in her own way. Such situation undermines accountability to community, which now impacts the sense of safeguard of care and justice. Church authorities seem to be inclined to protect the integrity of the ordained over the dignity and rights of church members. There appears to be a feeling by the Church hierarchy that the attitude or idea of having a conversation about the rot of the ecclesiastical structure may be more scandalous than the already visible scandal in the actions of the clergy. Hence the tendency to conceal obvious clergy boundaries trespassing. It remains to be said that abuse of this nature is simply beyond what the Church can handle internally; the Church in this case is an arbiter in her own case, a situation that will seldom have just and accountable adjudication.

Holding perpetrators accountable, whomever they may be, is a sure way of mitigating domestic violence in Nigeria by both church and state. Collaboration between the duo in this all-important project will produce a promising outcome.

Church and State Collaboration

Ultimately, the task of restoring the dignity and rights of abused women and children in Nigeria requires synergy between the state and church. This is because in part both have the power and authority to transform the dominant culture of violence. In addition, the recognition that religions shape societies[203] is particularly true of the Nigerian State. From the period of the colonial rule (1914-1960) until present, religion has been a dominant force in Nigerian politics and policymaking. At all levels of government, Muslims and Christians have always sought to have their religious interests represented even though sometimes to the detriment of nation building and national unity. The issue of domestic violence touches on fundamental rights of human persons irrespective of religious affiliation. This is one issue that religious leaders in Nigeria could have religion meaningfully play a significant role to shape and impact socio-political opportunities for the flourishing of their members and the citizenry. We therefore, expect the Catholic Church to rise to advocate government enactment and enforcement of laws that protect victims of domestic violence and punish or correct perpetrators. Collaboration with other church denominations, religious institutions and relevant agencies would be fruitful. Such advocacy is required to remind the government of her duty to her citizens. The state on her part cannot afford to ignore the role of the body of Christ as a moral au-

---

[203] Long and Lynch, *The Good Funeral*, 97.

thority in society. When the desired promulgation is made, it is expected that leadership (both civil and ecclesial) be subject to the laws. This would ensure the confidence of the people in their leaders and ultimately ensure the respect of the humanity of the vulnerable of society and promote good followership.

Further implication of the task of restoring the dignity and rights of domestic violence victims for the Nigerian state and church is the provision of resources for victims and survivors of domestic violence to help them on the trajectory of recovery. When victims decide to flee abusive relationships, where do they run to? Often, their parents are deceased and the women married into their maiden homes are not as friendly. What or who guarantees their safety even when they choose to stay in their maiden homes or be on their own? The establishment of shelters or a place of refuge for victims becomes necessary. Safe houses for domestic violence victims and survivors have been set up in a few states in the country by civil society organizations (CSOs) like WACOL, Project Alerts. Ensuring the building of shelters in most cities or communities across the federation by the Nigerian state (and the Church where possible) is a veritable way of mitigating abuse and safeguarding the dignity and rights of victims of domestic violence. Domestic violence is a threat to our common humanity and it requires an adequate and prompt ecclesial and leadership response to save persons, families, church and the Nigerian society from its pervasive grip. The Church's collaboration with the state captains is certainly crucial if the transformation of the current pervading narrative of domestic violence in Nigeria is to take place. The desired transformation that we expect to be facilitated by the church and state would bring about the healing, wholeness and empowerment of the numerous victims and survivors of domestic violence who look up to them for help.

SECTION III

SOCIAL TRANSFORMATION

CHAPTER NINE

COMPASSION-PRAXIS MINISTRY
FOR VICTIMS OF DOMESTIC VIOLENCE

Compassion and Human Suffering

The reality of human suffering reveals the vulnerability and brokenness of our common humanity. The experience of violence, abuse of human rights, and dehumanization of persons are blatantly evil and not only inflict pain on bodies of victims but also deface their spirit. Human suffering evokes different responses and attitudes such as indifference, as well as negative and positive emotions. Indifference or apathy often results from lack of awareness of the evil that brings about suffering. Suffering is unattractive to the human person, often repelling, and sometimes disgusting, thus leading to apathy. Such negative emotions as fear, envy and shame prevent us from connecting with those who suffer. Consequently, we end up not regarding others' pain as serious or worthy of our attention, blaming them for their suffering or pretending that their fate will never be our lot. Often people have responded with pity, sympathy or compassion to others' experience of violence and suffering. While pity and sympathy are expressions of concern, they produce little or no effects in the lives and circumstances of sufferers. However, compassion does.

Scholars of pastoral theology, political theology and ethics identify compassion as an appropriate and necessary response to human suffering especially suffering resulting from injustice. In their book,

Compassion: A Reflection on the Christian Life, Henri Nouwen, Donald McNeil, and Douglas Morrison argue that compassion is not our default as humans but a disposition that we are called to cultivate.[204] This is because of the attitude of indifference that manifest in the face of human suffering and more so the fact that most of what humans suffer are human evil. According to Wendy Farley, violence or human evil de-creates the human person and destroys their beauty, and in the face of its de-creating and devastating impact, compassion has the power to recreate.

> Compassion is the power that ignites the beauty of a soul after suffering has snuffed it out. Compassion is the kind of power that works on spirit and not on matter. It is not an impotent emotion of pity or even sympathy. It is not only companionship in misery. It is the name of a kind of power – the only kind of power – that redeems.[205]

Compassion, therefore, is an active force that is restorative and transformative. It is an expression of God's love, which he has manifested in his relationship with humankind. God is profoundly com-

---

[204] Henri Nouwen, Donald McNeil, and Douglas Morrison, *Compassion: A Reflection on the Christian Life* (New York: Doubleday, 1989), 4.

[205] Wendy Farley, "Evil, Violence, and the Practice of Theodicy," in *Telling the Truth: Preaching about Sexual and Domestic Violence,* ed. John McClure and Nancy Ramsay (Cleveland, OH: United Church Press, 1998), 15.

passionate and has no element of competition in him, unlike us humans. In the face of human suffering, the expectation is that we, like God, identify with those among us who suffer. Before we explore the dynamics of God's compassion and our vocation to be compassionate, let us explain what compassion is and what it is not.

Understanding Compassion

Compassion from the Latin *pati* and *cum* means "to suffer with." The Hebrew *rahamin* translates as compassion, mercy, affection and love. *Rahamin* comes from the same root as *rehem* which is translated as uterus, mother's womb, maternal covering of life or entrails.[206] It is a word, which evokes unconditional maternal love. This organ of the human body was considered the symbolic center of pity and compassion.[207] The word as used in the Old Testament with maternal connotations expresses God's actions that reveal his unconditional love for his people. The word, therefore, stands for both the physical organ of a female and a psychic state. To be compassionate means to express the sort of love that a woman feels for the child of her womb or entrails.

---

[206] Sofia Quispe, "The Connection with the Mercy and Compassion that Inhabits Us," in *Mercy*, Concilium Series, ed. Lisa Cahill, Diego Irarrazaval, and Joao Cha (London: SCM Press, 2017), 13-14.

[207] Martin Prudky, "Mercy," in *Encyclopedia of the Bible and its Reception*, ed. Constance M. Furey et al., vol. 18 (Boston: De Gruyter, 2020), 704.

Compassion presupposes that there is suffering and that someone or some people are suffering. It also presupposes that the suffering has a source and that there is someone standing out there who can and should intervene to alleviate or end the suffering. Compassion is the response of the bystander to the victim of suffering and/or to the structure that is responsible for the suffering. Compassion is a concrete action to identify with one who suffers; it is a conscious decision, which has to do with taking an effective action to right a wrong.[208]

It follows, therefore, that compassion is not a mere feeling of pity or sympathy for the suffering of others. Pitying or sympathizing with a victim of violence or suffering may make the one feel good for a while but does not restore what is lost, neither does it change nor end the cause of the suffering. Identifying with the misfortune of another in this case is experienced on the level of sensibility and thus is simply an emotion. Compassion is not a bending from a privileged stance toward the underprivileged; it is not a reaching out to the less fortunate below from on high. This is because the privileged person, in this case, remains undisturbed in their comfort zone and only reaches out conveniently and sparingly to the other. It carries with it little or no commitment, lacks the ability to share the space of victim, and is devoid of the will to transform the status quo. However, to be compassionate means to connect directly and concretely

---

[208] Quispe, "The Connection with the Mercy and Compassion that Inhabits Us," 13.

with the victim(s) of suffering. According to Nouwen, McNeil, and Morrison:

> Compassion asks us to go where it hurts, to enter into places of pain, to share in brokenness, fear, confusion, and anguish. Compassion challenges us to cry out with those in misery, to mourn with those who are lonely, to weep with those in tears. Compassion requires us to be weak with the weak, vulnerable with the vulnerable, and powerless with the powerless. Compassion means full immersion in the condition of being human.[209]

From the above explanation, it is clear that compassion involves awareness of suffering, an attitude of wanting to alleviate it and a choice to take action. Identifying with those in pain mitigates their pain, solidarity with the weak provides them strength, and standing by the vulnerable makes them secure and protected. Acting on behalf of the weak, powerless and vulnerable assures their empowerment and emancipation, and challenges the structure of suffering and evil. The action of immersion in the condition of the sufferer is an important expression of compassion. It is in God that we find a concrete expression of 'full immersion in the condition of being human.'[210] The Christian history is a narrative of the intervention of a merciful and compassionate God in the course of humanity's vulnerability, pain and helplessness.

---

[209] Nouwen, McNeil and Morrison, *Compassion*, 3-4.

[210] Nouwen, McNeil and Morrison, *Compassion*, 4.

Compassion or mercy is born in the reality of human misery. According to Thomas Aquinas, the encounter of love and misery gives birth to mercy, which finds its place in the very heart of Christianity.[211] Compassion in its perfect expression is found in God - "I desire mercy not sacrifice"[212] - who wills that we imbibe and practice compassion.

God as Compassionate

The biblical tradition identifies compassion or mercy as a pivotal attribute of God. In his dealings with humankind, God has demonstrated consistently a loving and caring disposition. God is a compassionate God and according to Farley, "[i]t is in the nature of God to be compassionate in all things"[213] Every action of God toward humans and the entire creation is seen from the prism of compassion and love. Klaus-Peter Adam, a professor of Old Testament, describes God's creation of the human person as an act of compassion. In an article titled "The Earth and the Earthling: Thoughts on Gen 2-3" he asserts that God demonstrated his tender care for humans at the beginning of human history through the acts of a potter and a gardener. God's art of forming man from the dust of the earth (Gen 2: 7) was an intimate, tangible, creative and thoughtful process. His

---

[211] Thomas Aquinas, *Summa Theologiae*, 2a, 2ae 30 quoted in *Encyclopedia of the Bible and Its Reception*, ed. Constance M. Furey et al., vol. 18 (Boston: De Gruyter, 2020), 725.

[212] Hos 6: 6; Mt 9: 13.

[213] Farley, "Evil, Violence, and the Practice of Theodicy," 15.

breathing into his nostrils the breath of life is a show of intimacy and devotion. In his role as a gardener, God provided the man and the woman a home in a rich garden. Even at the fall, God in his compassion provided them a resourceful care for the harsh reality of life outside the garden. For Adam, the provision of clothing for the fallen first humans (Gen 3:21) was an act of compassion in the face of the suffering they were about to undergo.[214]

From the foregoing, it is clear that Adam identifies God's love in the act of creation and thus affirms Farley's assertion that God manifests his compassion in all things. This love is not only that of a psychic state but an attribute he exercises in the concrete artisanal activity of forming the human person, bringing them into being, and supporting them in the face of the hard realities of life.

Jewish and Christian theology find in God's identification with those in need, a visible expression of his compassion for humanity. In both Old and New Testaments, scripture demonstrates that the image of a God who sides with those on the underside of power is a dominant theme. From the story of slavery in Egypt to the Babylonian exile, the striking and memorable narratives are those that tell a tale of a God who stands over against structures or systems of oppression.[215] God was moved to emancipate the Israelites under servitude in Egypt.

---

[214] Klaus-Peter Adam, "The Earth and the Earthling: Thoughts on Gen 2-3" in *Currents in Theology and Mission* 47, no. 1 (January 2020): 35-36.

[215] Jonathan Walton, *A Lens of Love: Reading the bible in its World for our World* (Louisville, KY: John Knox Press, 2018), 38.

I have indeed seen the misery of my people in Egypt. I have heard them crying for help on account of their taskmasters. Yes, I am aware of their sufferings. And I have come down to rescue them from the clutches of the Egyptians and bring them up out of that country, to a country rich and broad, to a country flowing with milk and honey.[216]

God therefore, has deep emotions for the victims of suffering and readily takes concrete steps to end their suffering. God sees, hears and knows the affliction of his people and consequently rises to action. According to Jonathan Walton, God's identification with the marginalized and victimized of society is indicative of his radical love for us.[217] One can say that the first word that God speaks in the face of human suffering is compassion.

In revelations of Godself, God did not leave us in doubt of his compassionate attribute. In his encounter with Moses on Mount Sinai while handing him over the Decalogue, God made a self-revelation of his identity as a God whose thousands-fold mercy is dominant compared to his fourfold anger:

And Yahweh descended in a cloud and stood with him there and pronounced the name Yahweh. Then Yahweh passed before him and called out 'Yahweh, Yahweh, God of tenderness and com-

---

[216] Ex 3: 7-8.

[217] Walton, *A Lens of Love*, 39.

passion, slow to anger, rich in faithful love and constancy, maintaining his faithful love to thousands, forgiving fault, crime and sin, yet letting nothing go unchecked, and punishing the parent's fault in the children and in the grandchildren to the third and fourth generation.[218]

Throughout the Old Testament, we come across the compassion and mercy of God to his people despite their disobedience as a constant refrain, and the politico-theological narrative of a compassionate God who intervenes in human history to ensure the people's liberation and the transformation of social injustice. This is by no means a way of ignoring the reality of divine violence found in the Old Testament. Such passages as Joshua 6-11 where God commanded the slaughter of the Canaanites have attracted historical-critical scholarship on the issue of divine violence, and presents a "dark side" of sacred scripture. While biblical scholars like Eryl Davies[219] have developed some exegetical and hermeneutical reading strategies for understanding the violent texts, we must admit with Simon Joseph that the Old Testament portrayal of God is ethically problematic. It raises the troubling questions about the nature of

---

[218] Ex 34: 5-7.

[219] Eryl Davies in his book *The Immoral Bible: Approaches to Biblical Ethics* identifies five distinct readings of the divine violent texts, namely evolutionary, cultural relativism, canonical, paradigmatic and reader-response criticism.

God in the biblical tradition, especially as this picture stands in contrast to key elements in the Jesus tradition,[220] which we shall discuss in the next chapter.

For the Hebrew prophets, God reveals his care for the most vulnerable in Israel under oppressive and highhanded leaders. Although they have their own distinct emphases and approaches, they all speak about God's predilection for the poor and oppressed and his indignation at unjust systems. Among others, Amos, Micah, Isaiah, and Jeremiah, are prominent in their denunciation of social injustice and oppression. Amos speaks about violent gains and oppression of the rich against the poor.[221] God sides the most vulnerable whenever the powerful "trample the head of the poor into the dust of the earth, and push the afflicted out of the way."[222] Walter Houston supposes possible coercion of the poor by the rich without ruling out the possibility of physical violence by the powerful in the time of the Hebrew prophets.[223] The political and religious leaders profited from the misery of the people and hence God threatened the annihilation of the city because of such corruption.[224] God addresses the oppressed (in Micah and Isaiah) as "my people" or "the

---

[220] Simon Joseph, *The Nonviolent Messiah: Jesus, Q, and the Enochic Tradition* (Minneapolis, MN: Fortress Press, 2014), 65-66.

[221] Am 3: 10.

[222] Am 2: 7.

[223] Walter Houston, *Contending for Justice: Ideologies and Theologies of Social Justice in the Old Testament* (New York: T&T Clark, 2006), 67.

[224] Mic 3: 12.

poor of my people."[225] According to Houston, these phrases under-
line God's personal relationship with and concern for the oppressed.
This also plays out in the allegorical context of Ezekiel 34, "my
sheep."[226]

The prophets are God's mouthpiece and instruments to announce his compassion and liberation of suffering humanity. Isaiah
announces God's commission to him:

> The spirit of Lord Yahweh is on me for Yahweh has anointed
> me. He has sent me to bring the news to the afflicted, to soothe
> the broken-hearted, to reclaim liberty to captives, release to
> those in prison, to proclaim a year of favor from Yahweh and a
> day of vengeance for our God, to comfort all who mourn, (to
> give to Zion's mourners), to give them for ashes a garland, for
> mourning-dress, the oil of gladness, for despondency, festal at-
> tire.[227]

The oracles of God manifested by God in his dealings with humanity from creation reached its full expression in Jesus who identifies himself as the fulfilment of the prophecies.[228] The next chapter
discusses the depth of God's love and compassion as revealed in the
person and earthly ministry of Jesus. In light of such ethics of compassion in the prophets, Ezekiel's vision of dry bones [Ez 37: 1-14] is

---

[225] Is 3: 15; Mic 2: 8-9.

[226] Houston, *Contending for Justice*, 87

[227] Is 61: 1-3.

[228] Lk 4: 16-21.

crucial. Out of compassion, the valleys of dry bones, the islands of death are transformed into valleys of new life.

It is equally important to mention that Jonah in his mission was scandalized by God's compassionate gesture toward the sinful nation that was in need of God's mercy. The prophet had expected God to destroy the great city of Nineveh but was disappointed at God's mercy. "Please, Yahweh, isn't this what I said would happen when I was still in my own country? That was why I first tried to flee to Tarshish, since I knew you were a tender, compassionate God, slow to anger, rich in faithful love, who relents about inflicting disaster"[229] God's compassion is universal and embraces all in need of his mercy wherever they are.

For Thomas Aquinas, compassion or mercy is not just one of God's attributes but his greatest virtue. This is because God does not give out of any need of his own, but gives purely and freely out of his own lovingly liberality and kindness.[230] The scholastic theologian asserts that God enacts his omnipotence primarily through God's omnipotent deeds of mercy, that is, in those activities, which only God can bring about. He gives us four examples of God's omnipotent deeds that display the richness of divine mercy, (which includes the creation of humans we mentioned earlier as acknowledged by Klaus-Peter Adam).

---

[229] Jon 4: 2.

[230] Aquinas, *Summa*, in *Encyclopedia of the Bible*, 725.

First, the act of creation is itself an omnipotent deed of supreme mercy for our non-existence, for when we could not even cry out for mercy, God in his mercy brought us into existence. Second, God in his mercy made us in his own image and likeness so that we might enjoy his own beatitude. Third, he mercifully recreated us when we were corrupted by sin and death. Fourth, such a renewal was accomplished by the merciful Father sending his only son."[231]

Catholic theology recognizes the mystery of the incarnation as the highest manifestation of God's compassion for humanity and the entire creation. Indeed, "Jesus Christ is and remains the most radical manifestation of God's compassion."[232] "For this is how God loved the world: he gave his only Son, so that everyone who believes in him may not perish but may have eternal life."[233] God revealed his compassion through the redemption wrought in his incarnate Son and in the incorruptible life that comes from his Spirit. As a compassionate God, he shares our joys and pain, defends and protects us, and willingly and readily suffers with us. God is moved by our pain and participates in the concrete human struggle.

From the biblical tradition, we see that the compassion of God is his way of justice and holiness, which is in connection with God's

---

[231] Thomas Aquinas, *Commentary on Ephesians,* quoted in *New Catholic Encyclopedia,* ed. Bernard L. Marthaler et al., 2nd ed. vol. 9 (Detroit: Gale, 2003), 507.

[232] Nouwen, McNeil and Morrison, *Compassion,* 50.

[233] Jn 3:16.

caring attitude to those who are suffering. Before we discuss the compassion of God as manifested in the life and work of Jesus, let us therefore, consider the justice of God in light of his compassionate nature.

The Justice of God

God's nature as revealed in the biblical tradition indicates that he is God of justice and righteousness. These attributes of justice and righteousness necessitate his taking offense at oppression and acts of injustice. The prophets treated injustice as a social and political theme. The oppressors belonged to a class and the oppressed to another. The prophets are consistent in asserting that the acts of injustice are offensive to God; God is the guarantor of justice and moves to punish the violation of justice.[234] The denunciation of evil or oppression leads to the pronouncement of judgment. The prophets pronounced God's judgement against the wealthy and powerful who had oppressed or failed to protect the rights of the poor.[235]

Like compassion, the concept of strict justice of God is a regular refrain in the Old Testament. The strict justice of God is a justice system that rewards only good actions and punishes only bad deeds.[236] Thus, in the Old Testament, there appears to be a distinction between justice as the salvific deliverance and justice as God's

---

[234] Houston, *Contending for Justice*, 93.

[235] Am 2: 6-7; Is 3: 13:-15: Jer 2: 34.

[236] Ex 34: 6-7; Deut 5: 9-10; Mic 7: 9; Si 5: 6-8.

wrath against the wicked. This has led to the understanding of the "justice of God," as either vindictive justice, that is, a measure whereby God punishes sinners, or as distributive justice, that is, the justice by which God chastises sinners and recompenses the just.[237] A misunderstanding of God's justice casts a shadow to divine compassion. Following the understanding of justice of God as his wrath against his creatures from the Old Testament, the Marcionites, Manicheans and Gnostics, for instance identify the God of the Old Testament as lacking in compassion unlike the God of the New Testament. For the Marcionites, the compassionate God is different from the God of judgment.[238] This dualism creates a problem.

Orthodox Christian theology, however, maintains that God is same and as both merciful and just. According to the Catholic teaching, "God is neither only just and not merciful, nor only merciful but not just, nor are there two Gods, one just and one merciful, as the dualistic trends maintained,"[239] and "God's justice does not conflict with his mercy, nor does his mercy diminish his justice. Both are part of God's absolute goodness."[240] The Christian understanding is that the justice of God makes it such that God acts mercifully towards sinners and God's mercy functions in accord with his justice.

---

[237] D. M Crossan and T G Weinandy, "Justice of God," in *The New Catholic Encyclopedia*, ed. Bernard L. Marthaler et al., 2nd ed. vol. 8 (Detroit, MI: Gale, 2003), 70.

[238] Eugene Ulrich, "Mercy," in *Encyclopedia of the Bible and its Reception*, ed. Constance M. Furey et al, vol.18 (Boston: De Gruyter, 2020), 724.

[239] Ulrich, "Mercy," 722.

[240] Crossant and Weinandy, "Justice of God," 72.

As Aquinas puts it: "mercy does not destroy justice, but in a sense is the fullness thereof."[241] God therefore, deals mercifully with human beings more than they justly merit and he mercifully punishes them less than they do justly deserve.

Houston does not find much of the strict justice of God in the Old Testament. The overarching refrain therein is the compassion of God, which is evident throughout the Old Testament texts including the prophets. He rather suggests that the suppression of this glaring attribute of the Old Testament God and the emphasis on the strict justice of God is as a result of poor scholarly reading.[242]

We can arguably assert that in the Old Testament, the justice of God is neither vindictive nor distributive but salvific, and it has its basis on God's commitment to his covenant with the people of Israel. God is just because God remains faithful to the promises of salvation and deliverance that he made. Thus, such theological terms as justice, salvation, fidelity and truth are easily used in the Old Testament interchangeably (Ps 97, 98.2-3, Dt 32.4).[243] The salvific plan

---

[241] Aquinas, *Summa*, in *Encyclopedia of the Bible*, 724.

[242] Houston argues that, The globalization of judgment in all the prophets, the use of the Exodus tradition as a reproach… cannot repress the compassion for the poor, the plain moral condemnation of injustice, and the sense of YHWH as the God of justice, which are the leading features of the oracles of judgment. Compassion for the poor may even be contradicted by the manner in which the judgment is conceived, but it still comes through and resounds in our reading of the texts.[242] (Houston, *Contending for Justice*, 95).

[243] Crossant and Weinandy, "Justice of God," 70.

of God prompted the incarnation that provided humanity the opportunity to experience a concrete expression of God's love in the person of his incarnate Son, Jesus Christ.

CHAPTER TEN

THE MINISTRY OF JESUS
AND THEOLOGIES OF COMPASSION

Compassion in the life and ministry of Jesus

The incarnation reveals the depth of God's love for vulnerable humanity. The incarnation is a self-emptying, a condition of powerlessness that is beyond human intellectual and emotional grasp. Jesus, the invisible God made visible[244] not requiring to experience the human condition freely chose to do so simply out of love. The Word was made flesh and dwelt among us.[245] The mystery of God-with-us is a concretization of the fullness of God's compassion for us. It is a true expression of a full and unreserved absorption in the condition of being human by the divine. The life and ministry of Jesus embody a compassionate, merciful and life-giving God. Jesus is a definite and tangible embodiment of God's compassion for humanity. During his earthly sojourn, he "went about doing good,"[246] reaching out to men and women, low and high. The message of the reign of God (which was central to his teaching) he preached to everyone in order to save as many as possible.

---

[244] Col 1:15.

[245] Jn 1: 14.

[246] Acts 10: 38.

A distinguishing characteristic of the life and ministry of Jesus is his compassionate disposition. Jesus related to those who encountered him out of care and love for their flourishing. He responded to the hungry, deaf, dumb, blind, crippled, lepers, widows, bereaved, and possessed who came to him with their suffering and pain out of the divine compassion that made him to assume human nature. He equally related with leading Jewish personalities with compassionate heart.[247] Beneath the cures and interventions that he made in people's lives, is the profound compassion that moved him to action. The expression "moved with compassion" appears twelve times in the Gospels and was used in reference to Jesus or his Father. It explains the deep and compelling tenderness that God has and expresses toward his creation. Divine compassion transforms human condition from a cause of despair into a source of hope.[248]

The gospels, no doubt, contain some elements of violence as invoked by Jesus. Jesus did say, contrary to popular expectation, that he has come not to bring peace but sword and strife (Mt 10: 34-36), and asked his disciples to get swords ready (Lk 22:36-38), which lead to the question of whether Jesus is a violent revolutionary. Scholars differ on this question and there are reasons to associate him with revolution and reasons not to. One may be inclined however, to reason with Daniel Harrington, for instance, that the evangelist Matthew, after the beatitude on peacemakers (5:9) and the invitation to

---

[247] Mk 5: 21-24, 35-43; Lk 14: 1; 7:36; Jn 3:1-21.

[248] Nouwen, McNeil, and Morrison, *Compassion*, 14-15.

love one's enemies (6:44) could hardly have understood Jesus' saying in 10:34 as a call for a warfare. The words of Jesus here rather, according to Harrington, highlight the division among people that follow consequentially as a decision for or against the gospel.[249] This aligns with Charles Sigel and Mitchell Mackinem's hermeneutic of Lk 22:36-38. Like most scholars, they invite readers to understand Jesus' instruction to his disciples as they entered into Jerusalem to have swords ready in a figurative sense. The sword signifies opposition and Jesus was only telling his followers to gird their loins for opposition.

> The sword was the tool of division and opposition. Nobody in Jerusalem would have seen the sword as simply a tool of war. The sword as a harbinger of division is a common image in the Bible. Therefore, when Jesus tells them to prepare and buy a sword, he was trying to communicate that opposition and danger lay ahead.[250]

We thus observe that dominant in Jesus' life, ministry and death is his compassionate and nonviolent personality.

As obvious from its Latin root, compassion means to suffer with the other. The sufferer is always at the receiving end of pain or evil. To be compassionate therefore, implies identifying with sufferers in

---

[249] Daniel Harrington, *The Gospel of Matthew*, Sacra Pagina Series, vol. 1 (Collegeville, PA: The Liturgical Press, 1991), 150.

[250] Charles Sigel and Mitchell Mackinem, *Did He Say That? The Difficult Words of Jesus* (Eugene, OR: Wipf & Stock, 2016), 55.

their adversity. Jesus gave expression to his genuine compassion for humanity by his solidarity with the *hoi polloi* of society. He pitched his tent with the sick, handicapped, outcasts, sinners, and women. He did so, to provide them dignity, liberation and freedom. The Hebrews up to the time of Jesus identified certain diseases with sin and uncleanness. Leprosy, blindness and hemorrhage could be because of one's sin or that of one's parents (Jn 9: 2) and these suffice to declare sufferers as unclean. Lepers were quarantined and lived in isolation outside the camp.[251] There was the belief that suffering and sickness are a divine punishment for sin committed by persons.[252] The belief in individuals' contamination with sin even from their mother's womb was not uncommon. It was also held that children inherit or suffer the consequences of the parent's sins.[253] In this scenario, it becomes clear that people who suffered from diseases not only suffered from physical pain; they were subjected also to emotional pain, isolation, neglect, discrimination, rejection, ostracism, and spiritual abuse. Those afflicted with the ritually impure ailments were considered unclean consequently not given a place in society, especially in relation to the temple.[254]

As a concerned Jewish religious figure, Jesus identified with the common Jewish people. Jesus lived in a time when there were several

---

[251] Lev 13: 46; Num 5: 2-3.

[252] Job 4: 7-9; Jn 9:2.

[253] Ex 20: 5; 34: 7; Num 14: 18.

[254] Wati Longchar, "Unclean and Compassionate Hand of God," *The Ecumenical Review* 63, no. 4 (December 2011): 415.

sectarian groups seeking to influence the religious views and practical behavior of ordinary Palestinian Jews.[255] Among the sects were the Pharisees who from the evangelists' accounts had the most encounter with Jesus. The Pharisees were concerned with correct behavior and correct interpretation of the law and had consequently a prominence for their accurate or precise interpretation of the Mosaic Law.[256] Though some of the encounters with these religious and political groups seem conflictual, we find in Jesus' attitude to the people and to Judaism a humane and compassionate approach meant to draw them to their God. Jesus had a vision and mindset about the consummation of Israel's history and the way to lead her to this end. Like the Pharisees, he reached out to common people and drew the attention of large crowds that followed him.

Undoubtedly, the Pharisees and Jesus shared a common belief in God's election of Israel, his gift of the Law, the need for the people to observe the Law in their everyday lives, and God's faithful guidance of Israel through history to a future consummation that involves Israel's restoration. Both possibly shared a belief in a final judgment, the resurrection of the dead, and in a kind of eschatological or messianic figure of God's agent at the end of time.[257] Each

---

[255] There were the Qumranites who were withdrawn to the desert, the Essenes that lived in their conventicles, the Sadducees that constituted a relatively small priestly and aristocratic group, and the Pharisees who endeavored to teach ordinary Jews their beliefs.

[256] John Meier, *A Marginal Jew: Rethinking the Historical Jesus*, vol. 3 (New York: Doubleday, 2001), 314.

[257] Meier, *A Marginal Jew*, vol.3, 338.

however, appears to have a different mindset on how the whole narrative of God's people is to be played out. Aware of this diversity of mindsets in the Jewish worldview at the time, N.T. Wright recognizes that Jesus was opposed to first century Judaism, including Pharisaism, as deviating from Israel's God and commands.[258]

Wright identifies in Jesus' welcome to sinners and the marginalized population of his time as one of the areas of deviation, which the religious leaders found offensive. According to him, objection and conflict with Jesus' practice did not arise simply because he was preaching and demonstrating love and compassion as if the Jewish culture and religion opposed such practices; it was not so much so that Jesus was propagating a different religious system. Jesus was offering a new world order, the end of Israel's desolation and the inauguration of the reign of God.

> [H]e [Jesus] was offering this final eschatological blessing outside the official structures, to all the wrong people, and on his own authority. That was his offence...it was about the scandalous implied redefinition of the kingdom itself. Jesus was replacing adherence or allegiance to Temple and Torah with allegiance to himself. Restoration and purity were to be had, not through the usual channels, but through Jesus.[259]

---

[258] N.T. Wright, *Jesus and the Victory of God* (Minneapolis, MN: Fortress Press, 1996), 93.

[259] Wright, *Jesus,* 272,274.

While John Meier may not agree with Wright in submitting that Jesus' identification with the Jewish peasants was a source of conflict (the Pharisees were also reaching out to them with their teaching), he would agree that Jesus had an approach different from his contemporaneous religious leaders. Meier sees in Jesus not a systematic teacher, rabbi or scribe like any of his contemporaries. Jesus is a religious charismatic. As a religious charismatic, he does not consider himself as requiring to derive his teaching from the traditional authority; he rather knows directly and intuitively God's will in any given situation or issue. Jesus assumes the prophetic role of gathering the people of God (all Israel), and preparing them for the reign of God; he and he alone can tell Israel how to interpret and practice God's Law as it pertains to the members of the kingdom.[260] Obviously, Jesus espouses a moderate and pragmatic personality and ministry that appears more attractive than the rigorism of the religious teachings of the religious sects of his time.

This compassionate association with the *hoi polloi*, sinners, and the ritually impure led Jesus to become a fellow sufferer. To intimately suffer with them and *ipso facto* alleviate human suffering, Jesus accepted the supposedly infamous suffering and death on the cross. The cross signifies the cruelest kind of suffering. It demonstrates Jesus' identification with all who suffer various kinds of ills. He himself committed no crime yet he had to suffer and in this way

---

[260] John Meier, *A Marginal Jew: Rethinking the Historical Jesus*, vol. 4 (New Haven, CT: Yale University Press, 2009), 415.

he identified with all those who suffer ignominy and injustice, rejection and discrimination from others. Thus, the cross represents the suffering of innocent persons and an emblem of solidarity with all sufferers especially those who are socially dislocated. This is chiefly the import of the cross.[261] In the kenosis lies a concrete demonstration of Jesus' (God's) compassion for us. Jesus "not only suffered our painful human condition in all its concreteness but also suffered death with us in one of its rawest, ugliest, and most degrading forms. It was a death that we "normal" human beings would hardly be willing to consider ours."[262]

It will be important to discuss the significance of the kenosis in our lives and circumstances. Before that however, let us examine Jesus' understanding of the Law. Jesus favored the spirit of law, which bespeaks compassion while his contemporaries emphasizing the externals, settled, as it were, for the letter of the law.

Jesus' Interpretation of the Law

Law plays a huge role in the life of people and society and so it was not possible for Jesus to be indifferent to its observance and impact on the lives of the people he came to redeem. The gospels and non-canonical literature indicate that there were competing views or interpretations of the law by various Jewish groups at the time of

---

[261] Longchar, "Unclean and Compassionate Hand of God," 416.
[262] Nouwen, McNeil, and Morrison, *Compassion*, 24.

Jesus. The gospels provide enough evidence to demonstrate that Jesus had conflicts with the political and religious leaders of his time. The Pharisees and the Sadducees were active Jewish political-religious groups at the time. Jesus' encounters with the Sadducees, Pharisees and scribes always presented scenarios of disagreements and tensions. The controversies usually pertained to difference in understanding and application of the law. According to Meier, the conflict between Jesus and the Pharisees over issues of the law reflects a larger struggle in the turn of the era over the correct interpretation of the Mosaic Law. Differences over the interpretation and practical consequences of the law (and temple worship) gave the Pharisees, Sadducees and other Jewish groups (like the Qumran) their distinctive identity.[263] So was Jesus; his own interpretation of same laws gave him a distinctness.

Some scholars depict Jesus as a cynic who opposed and subverted the Jewish laws and customs and all the religious boundaries of the second temple Judaism; some present him as a religious radical who rose against the oppressive priestly and Pharisaic purity regulations of his time, yet others see him as introducing purity ideology that is hardly Jewish.[264] The Jewish laws, including the purity laws, express the basic ideologies of the Jewish society at the time and Jesus in his ministry came up with an approach to the Mosaic

---

[263] Meier, *A Marginal Jew*, vol. 3, 315.

[264] Jonathan Klawans, "Moral and Ritual Purity" in *The Historical Jesus in Context*, ed. Amy-Jill Levine, Dale Allison and John Crossan (Princeton, NJ: Princeton University Press, 2006), 267.

Law that aligns with his vision of the reign of God and God's will for his people.

Far from rejecting the Sabbath law, Jesus embraced its observance but from a different approach. Jesus, as in Lk 13:15, far from opposing the Sabbath,

> wished instead to make the Sabbath livable for severely pressed Jewish peasants, who could hardly afford to stand by when they were in danger of losing one of their livestock, to say nothing of their children. Jesus' espousal of a pragmatic, down-to-earth approach to these questions reflects his desire to shield ordinary pious Jews from the attraction of sectarian rigorism.[265]

Meier describes such moderate and humane attitude to the law as "Jesus' commonsense approach"[266] to the Sabbath law. For Jesus, the human person is at the center of law. Sabbath is made for humans and not vice versa. This is part of Jesus' vision to restore the goodness in creation as originally willed by God in the beginning. This is an eschatological viewpoint from which he seeks to put things in their proper perspectives. Creation is at the origin of the Sabbath; this creation is meant to serve the good of humans created

---

[265] Meier, *A Marginal Jew*, vol.4, 296.

[266] Meier, *A Marginal Jew*, vol. 4, 296.

by God in the beginning and now restored by God in the later days.[267]

Jesus however, prohibited the divorce (Mk 10: 2-12) and oath (Mt 5: 34-37) laws unlike other Jewish sectarians of his time but had a detailed teaching on purity laws.[268] Jesus demonstrated his concern over moral rather than ritual laws in the Markan episode. Meier who distinguishes four categories of purity laws[269] maintains that Jesus was silence on matters concerning the ritual purity laws. According to him, for Jesus, ritual purity is not only not a pressing issue; it is not an issue at all.[270] His vision and personality as a charismatic prophet explains his indifference to ritual impurity. Meier argues that Mk 7:1-23 is a redaction of the evangelists with only vv. 10-12 (which referenced the Mosaic Law) as authentic words of the historical Jesus. Jonathan Klawans however, sees the passage not so much as a matter of redaction as it is about Jesus' emphasis and prioritization of one thing over another. Jesus, he argues, far from rejecting the Jewish purity laws, prioritized moral purity over ritual purity.[271] We consider this attitude of Jesus as a humane interpretation of the law flowing from his compassionate personality.

---

[267] Meier, *A Marginal Jew*, vol.4, 296.

[268] Mk 7: 1-23.

[269] John Meier makes four categories of purity laws namely, ritual (birth, sex, death), moral (murder and serious sexual sins), genealogical (marriage with the gentiles), and dietary laws.

[270] Meier, *A Marginal Jew*, vol.4, 414.

[271] Klawans, "Moral and Ritual Purity," 281.

Ultimately, Jesus' legal interpretative lens has its basis on a theology wherein God is primarily a God of compassion, action, and in solidarity with the *hoi polloi*. God is attentive to human pain and need; his will is, fundamentally, that of redemption and human flourishing. It is from this perspective that Jesus evaluated the law. Donald Senior and Carroll Stuhlmueller are in no doubt about Jesus' humane attitude to the law. They observe that Jesus himself was undoubtedly a strict Jew but there were instances where he summoned up his own authority and his own experience to put values of compassion and inner integrity in direct confrontation with the way his opponents' interpreted the law.[272] Such examples are the instances in the gospels where he challenged his contemporaries' narrow legalistic positions. Jesus puts love and compassion above any religious norms and rituals that downplayed the humanity of any category of people. God's compassionate hand manifested in love takes precedence over any religious norms and rituals.

Jesus demonstrated that no kind of disease could be categorized as a disease of sinners. For him, there is no connection between sin and infirmity; to stigmatize and to deny others the right to life, association or worship is sinful. Jesus never considered any disease or any human suffering condition to be outside the limits of his compassion, love and redemption. For him, every created person is precious and priceless, and has therefore to be cared for, cherished and protected. While the hermeneutics of the law by his cotemporary sectarian Jews reflected their understanding of the hope and

---

[272] Senior, *The Biblical Foundations for Mission*, 148.

worldview of some Jew people at the turn of the era, Jesus' interpretation of same laws reflects a compassionate attitude that respects human dignity and rights of all, and guarantees the integration of everyone in society and in the house of God. We find in his healing episodes the underlying motive of the health and flourishing of beneficiaries. As far as Jesus is concerned, any practices that fail to take into account the wholeness and flourishing of human subjects are not of God and therefore, stand to be changed.

The greatest law for Jesus therefore, is the law of love; as such all other laws are to be subordinated to the love command.[273] His life and ministry indicate and invite the transformation of human attitudes and structures in the light of this overarching divine purpose for humanity. The love of God and of one's neighbor is the meaning or basis of the law and the prophets.[274] So stated Jesus was not revising the law but was saving it from fallacious applications and desiring a hearing of the law in the spirit of the law.[275] The measure of keeping the law of love is being compassionate as God himself is.

Be Compassionate as God Is Compassionate (Lk 6: 36)

As deducible from the forgoing, the life and ministry of Jesus attest concretely that God is a compassionate God. This is the good

---

[273] Mt 22: 40; Mk 12:31; Lk 10:25-37.

[274] Mt 22: 40.

[275] Mark Elliot, "The Character of the Biblical God," in *The Identity of Israel's God in Christian Scripture*, ed. Don Collett et al. (Atlanta: The Society of Biblical Literature, 2020), 50.

tiding that suffering humanity blessedly has to their favor; God-with-us considers nothing human as alien to himself and lives in solidarity with us. Jesus is a servant God who washes our feet and unreservedly heals our wounds; he is an obedient God who listens and responds to needy humanity with love without measure.[276] In companionship with himself, Jesus calls us to be compassionate as our loving God is compassionate.[277] In and through him, becoming effective and vigorous ambassadors of God's compassion and signs of hope in a world acquainted with suffering and despair becomes attainable.

Pope Francis, who in his pontificate harps on God's attribute of mercy, asserts that all humans of any societal status share in God's love. "No one is excluded from life's hope, from God's love. The Church is sent to reawaken this hope everywhere, especially where it has been suffocated by difficult and oftentimes inhuman living conditions."[278] The pope recognizes that a considerable population of people in various societies have their hope of living and being loved suffocated by atrocious living conditions. The call to be compassionate like God becomes a call to lend a helping hand, to extend love to those who only have a dim hope of living a flourishing life so that they can breathe and not have their hope suffocate. Commenting on Jesus' compassion for the people he found to be like sheep without a shepherd (Mt 9:35-36), Pope Francis explains that in this

---

[276] Nouwen, McNeil, and Morrison, *Compassion*, 43.

[277] Lk 6: 36.

[278] Francis, *Walking with Jesus: A Way Forward for the Church* (Chicago: Loyola Press, 2015), 82.

way Jesus summons us to comprehend the depths of his heart, what he feels for the throng, and for all those he meets: that inner attitude of "compassion"; seeing the crowds, he felt compassion for them. In our time and contexts, the helpless crowds are the peoples of the various nations of the world who face various difficult life situations.[279] It is the mission of the Church to keep the hope of the suffering members of the human family alive by offering them mercy and compassion. For the Roman Pontiff, the invitation to mercy and compassion is pivotal to the ministry of Jesus and crucial to the church's mission. Commenting on the impulse of mercy from the biblical tradition and catholic theology, Sophia Quispe writes:

> I think that mercy and compassion lead us to the urgent need to heal, not only relationships, but the very conception of being human, which nurtures the longings for 'a new heaven and a new earth'. That means travelling on the paths that create different ways of life, with ways of acting that are much more life-giving and liberating, as Jesus did in facing up to the powers of his time, without worrying about being labelled 'impure' and dying as a result. It means taking the personal and communal paths and forms of resistance that stand up to all the powers by looking for Life with Dignity, Abundant Life, Living Well and Living Well Together.[280]

---

[279] Francis, *Walking With Jesus*, 105.

[280] Quispe, "The Connection with the Mercy and Compassion," 19.

The call to compassion envisions a life of dignity and flourishing for all. Compassion desires and strives for collaboration among people to acknowledge and work to restore the humanity of the wounded and powerless members of the human family. The element of solidarity with sufferers and ensuring their liberation are pivotal to contemporary theologies of compassion.

Solidarity and the Theologies of Compassion

Drawing from the biblical tradition, modern scholars in the areas of pastoral theology, political theology and ethics have developed theologies of compassion in response to suffering and injustice in our world. Human suffering acquires a place at the center of theology. Beyond mere pity, compassion invokes the appreciation of the 'other' as the concrete other. In the 'I-Thou' relationship when the 'other' is seen as a concrete entity like the 'I', one is able to perceive the harm and damage that suffering, especially that resulting from injustice, does to other's life. This awareness necessitates a response. The suffering of the other therefore, makes the practice of solidarity inevitable.

From the pastoral theological viewpoint, compassion is a vocation. According to Nouwen, McNeil and Morrison, through the incarnation, God shares our lives in solidarity. The call to participate in God's life is also an invitation to share in his compassionate attribute. The authors identify the vocation to compassion as central to the Christian life. Because being human and being compassionate are not the same, the call to be compassionate demands a total conversion of heart; it is a radical call that touches the core of our being. It requires a "voluntary displacement" that takes us out from our comfort zones to "places where people hurt and where we can experience with them our common human brokenness and our common need for healing."[281]

In a similar vein, Kroeger and Nason-Clark recognize that compassion involves a displacement from where we are to share in the space of our suffering brethren with the hope of showing understanding of their plight. Accordingly, "the Christian call to compassion is first and foremost a call to meet people where they are, to see the reality of their plight, to hear the cry of their heart and to attempt to understand their pain."[282] Speaking from the point of view of the experience of domestic violence, the authors submit that victims of abuse require the mending of their broken hearts, and describe the show of compassion as Christian love in action and a veritable means of heart mending. As Farley rightly says, and as we shall discuss in the following chapters, the work of compassion, that is, love in action as shown to abused persons include: sanctuary, pastoral counseling, support groups, legislative action, the intimacy and fun of friendship.[283]

A crucial element of solidarity with those in suffering and pain is the component of community effort. Following the early Christian

---

[281] Nouwen, McNeil, and Morrison, *Compassion*, 62.

[282] Kroeger and Nason-Clark, *No Place for Abuse*, 82.

[283] Farley, "Evil, Violence, and the Practice of Theodicy," 17.

community life and ministry, it is clear that compassion is not simply an individual's trait but the way of life of a community. We experience the presence of Christ in the life of the community. Life together in the faith community, therefore, ought to make us open and receptive to the affliction of others and to extend a compassionate hand to them. The community ought to be a place of compassion. It ought to be ready and willing to "experience and express their compassionate solidarity with those in whom the brokenness of the human condition [is] most visible."[284] For Kroeger and Nason-Clark, both the individual Christian and the faith community have the obligation to apply the healing balm of Gilead to soothe the wounds of our afflicted brethren.

> When the Christian church sets about bathing our lives, we do not feel dirty or shameful any longer. The old nature, replete with heartache and pain, is replaced with a new nature fashioned in likeness to Christ. The past is washed away. God's Spirit beckons us to start over – to mourn no longer, to rise and go forth, to put our hand to the plow and not look back.[285]

The above statement describes the transformation that takes place when we heed to the Christian call to compassion. From the old wounded nature springs up a new and transformed nature filled with new energy and vitality. We must however, recognize that

---

[284] Nouwen, McNeil, and Morrison, *Compassion*, 66.

[285] Kroeger and Nason-Clark, *No Place for Abuse*, 85.

transformation following the psychological and spiritual bruises of abuse does not heal instantly or magically. It takes a long time to heal and for the victims to experience the new nature or life that Kroeger and Nason-Clark are talking about. Farley, equally from the pastoral theological perspective, is a strong believer in the healing power of compassion. Farley however insists that the re-creating power of compassion does not come easy. "Recreating spirit occurs within the condition of finitude, within the psychosomatic, social complexity of personhood. This transformation is long and slow. The power of compassion can wash the rock of a heart for many decades before the heart softens and the effect be discerned."[286] The use of the metaphor "the rock of a heart" by Farley to refer to the heart of the afflicted bespeaks the gravity of the harm inflicted on the human heart by suffering and violence. All the same, Farley believes that the power of compassion is so strong to restore or re-create a wounded soul.

We can infer further that compassion does not consist only in solidarity or pastoral care of the afflicted. Solidarity with the wounded comprises also of condemning the structure responsible for the suffering. Indeed, the remembrance of Abel leads to the remembrance of Cain. Identifying with others in the suffering implies rising against the source of the pain and this can be confrontational.

We are inclined to associate compassion with actions by which wounds are healed and pains are relieved. But in a time in

---

[286] Farley, "Evil, Violence, and the Practice of Theodicy," 17.

which many people can no longer exercise their human rights, millions are hungry, and the whole human race lives under the threat of nuclear holocaust, compassionate action means more than offering help to the suffering. The power of evil has become so blatantly visible in individuals as well as in the social structures that dominate their lives that nothing less than strong and unambiguous confrontation is called for. Compassion does not exclude confrontation. On the contrary, confrontation is an integral part of compassion. Confrontation can indeed be an authentic expression of compassion."[287]

Indeed, honest and direct confrontation is a right and expected response born out of compassion. In avowing compassion for our suffering brethren, we ought to be ready to unmask the illusion of power, challenge idolatry, fight oppression and exploitation, and confront the perpetrators of these evils. To suffer with the poor, we must be willing to confront those individuals and systems that are responsible for impoverishing others. This is what it means to be compassionate. It is lips service to embark on liberating the captives whereas we are not prepared to dare those in possession of the prison keys. We cannot truly avow our solidarity with the oppressed without the resolve to challenge the oppressor. Compassion devoid of confrontation may become a pointless emotional commiseration.[288]

---

[287] Nouwen, McNei,l and Morrison, *Compassion*, 122.
[288] Nouwen, McNeil, and Morrison, *Compassion*, 123.

Also from the ethical dimension, compassion arouses the desire to challenge the status quo. Coming from the field of political ethics, Hille Haker describes compassion as "an emotional response that ideally translates into the motivation to action."[289] The action initiated by such moral emotion is likened to an outrage. In this sense, compassion "is akin to an outrage: it disrupts states of injustice, and it may therefore be expressed in outcries of anger and rage about the suffering of others."[290] Compassion as the sense of solidarity with the *hoi polloi* of society is therefore, a matter of justice. Compassion is a response to the injustice that plague the human society. It is the impulse that moves us to speak out without fear and to "*witness* against injustice; it imposes upon us the obligation to *resist* complicity in the harming of others, and to *seek the transformation of injustice to justice*."[291] From both practical theology and political ethics, compassion is an obligation, which requires us to identify with our suffering brethren and for their sake confront the unjust structures that deprive fellow moral agents their well-being and freedom.

Because of the reality of structural injustice and structures of violence in societies, it becomes a moral duty for Christians in the face of global moral evil, to stand for all victims of injustice. Morality, maintains Haker, "is a *demand* to include in one's striving for a good

---

[289] Hille Haker, "Compassion for Justice," in *Mercy,* Concilium Series, ed. Lisa Cahill, Diego Irarrazaval, and Joao Cha (London: SCM Press, 2017), 57.

[290] Haker, "*Compassion for Justice,*" 59.

[291] Haker, "*Compassion for Justice*", 57-8

life the others' suffering, especially when it stems from injustices."[292] Similar to Haker's concept of compassion and justice is Martha Nussbaum's idea of political love. In her exploration of the import of love and compassion on political ethics, Nussbaum maintains that political love enables moral agents to be compassionate and to live up the demands of justice.[293] According to the author, it is love that helps us to overcome the culture of indifference to injustices and sufferings, and envy, fear and shame, which are enemies of compassion. Nussbaum proposes an imaginative engagement of people and gathering them together around a set of common values via arts as a way of eschewing indifference. While Nussbaum's position is laudable for its emphasis on imagination and aesthetics, it may be too optimistic to be feasible especially for societies like Nigeria and most African nations where violence and injustice are deeply cultural and systemic. With Haker, however, we consider a resistant approach and a transformative solidarity in the face of indifference and other enemies of compassion.

Politically speaking, compassion is necessary to instill respect for the other and to acknowledge the suffering of any member(s) of society. It involves awareness of, remembering, denouncing and transforming the suffering. Thus, the likening of the ethics of compassion to the ethics of recognition and responsibility. According to Haker, "[t]he *Christian* political ethics of recognition and responsibility is a

---

[292] Haker, "*Compassion for Justice*", 60.

[293] Martha Nussbaum, *Political Emotions: Why Love Matters for Justice* (Cambridge, MA: The Belknap of Harvard University Press, 2013), 380-81.

political ethics of remembrance and witnessing, connecting the present compassionate, neighbourly love both with Jesus' teachings in the past and with the eschatological hope of divine justice."[294] We bear witness to the compassionate life and teaching of Jesus by recognizing the suffering of others among us. In doing so, we look forward to God's justice which is predicated upon our witnessing to the Christian life at the end. Haker therefore, maintains that awareness of the eschatological dimension of justice helps us to be mindful of the coming divine judgement.

> Without this anticipated judgement, we may well continue to love our country and *be*, at the same time, indifferent when the poor starve, migrants die, innocent people are killed by our very state, or millions of people are abandoned in prisons. Without a theology of judgement that is the other side of the compassion for justice, we may well uphold the international legal and political order that kills, daily, thousands of people. Those, however, who do share their bread and their homes with those in need are the witnesses of faith, they are the hope for those who have no hope.[295]

We must appreciate Haker's eschatological ethics. We recognize the fact that many Christians based on their church doctrines have

---

[294] Haker, *Compassion for Justice*, 60.
[295] Haker, *Compassion for Justice*, 61.

formed their consciences in such a manner that their actions are determined by their hope of heaven and the fear of God's judgment and of hell. Such eschatological hope and fear inform their actions for good and charitable works. Haker thus alludes to Christian teaching on eschatology, predicated on the idea of unjust and imperfect humanity in the face of just and perfect God.

> Within our sinful world the misuse of power, or greed, or lust, or hatred and prejudice cause horrendous and appalling injustice by violating the authentic dignity and just rights of human beings. Because this world's justice cannot possibly make right such injustices, Christians look then to the day when Jesus will come in glory for finally he will redress all wrongs and set all things right.[296]

It is important to recognize that in order to engage human suffering and violence meaningfully, we must confront the structures of injustice that impugn human dignity and rights. This does not involve simply invoking religious emotions especially realizing the secular character of society and pluralism of faiths. Injustice and violence are to be seen as evil in themselves considering the harm they do to persons concretely in the here and now; and as Tran observes, they are an attack on our common humanity.[297] As such, justice would entail acknowledging the humanity of all with their attendant

---

[296] Crossant and Weinandy, "Justice of God," 72.

[297] Tran, *Reset the Heart*, 24-25.

dignity and rights. Yet, Haker's theology of judgment is crucial in considering compassion for justice, recognizing that she writes from Christian ethical perspective. One could say that her ethics and theology come from a hope-based conviction: "that violence (and suffering) challenges our Christian communities to regenerate radical forms of prophetic, (pro)tested faith, and to hone those skills and instincts through public conscientization and participatory action, whose goal is insurrectional, resurrectional hope."[298]

The idea of public conscientization and participatory action, as espoused by Mai-Anh Le Tran becomes imperative for the church community and society in the face of violence especially violence that occur in the home. Thomas Groome, a practical theologian, developed a participatory praxis as a veritable tool for group conscientization and transformation.[299] The praxis is not only a form of solidarity with those who suffer but also a means through which victims of suffering can attain emancipation and human flourishing. Compassion-praxis oriented seminary formation and pastoral ministry are inevitable.

---

[298] Tran, *Reset the Heart*, 10.

[299] Thomas Groome developed Shared Christian Praxis (SCP) as a pedagogy for religious education and pastoral ministry. The SCP has 5 movements: Naming the present action, critical reflection, presenting/accessing the Christian Story and Vision (CSV), appropriating the CSV, and decision and response.

CHAPTER ELEVEN

SEMINARY FORMATION AND PARISH MINISTRY

Formed to Form

What I consider one of the richest traditions of the seminary I attended in Nigeria is the 'Tu es visit'. It is the visit made by the recently graduated theology students to their alma mater in gratitude for their training and ordination. The two-day visit is loaded with social and spiritual activities that involve the staff, seminarians and the newly ordained priest visitors. The program is informal and interactive and seminarians are served a rare sumptuous meal. Year after year during the eight years of my academic and formative program, there is one recurrent experience that the visitors share during the interactive forum which I came to realize its veracity in my own days as a newly ordained. The newly ordained priests expressed the challenge of the gulf between the seminary training and the concrete pastoral ministry. The academic and theoretical learning environment is contrasted sharply with the practical ministerial situations that confront the young and energetic priest. I recall that the priest formators in response validated the experience of the visiting young priests and explained that it was normal and was a matter of time. I think that the formators are not wrong totally in trying to build confidence in the nascent priests and in the bid to let them accept the situation as normal. Beginnings are not always smooth and we acquire certain knowledge by experience on the job. Nevertheless, one would expect more from the staff crew. My gut is that such a recurring question should have prompted them to ask the question: what shall we do to bridge the gap between the seminary curriculum/pedagogy and the pastoral ministry in the local context? When we do the same thing and get the same unsatisfactory result, a repeat of it is far from being wisdom.

The questions about curriculum and pedagogy, therefore, are crucial in the training of candidates for the priesthood. How could the seminary curriculum better reflect the local contexts that future ministers of the Word and sacraments work? How can the seminaries prepare the future priests who will minister in a violent society and among the violated and violators? What indeed does it mean to educate in a society marked by violence? For the four years of my theological studies in my alma mater, Pastoral Theology was never taught in class. There was nothing near practical theological studies in the curriculum. We had fair teaching and learning on the Scripture, Moral and Systematic theology as well as the liturgical tutoring on priestly Eucharistic ministerial practice. The training lacked a fair pastoral dimension. I am talking about a Post- *Pastores Dabo Vobis* era of seminary formation.[300] What we had as implicit curriculum was personal experiences of the priest professors. Again, these expe-

---

[300] *Pastores Dabo Vobis* (1992) was the first papal document on formation of priests that emphasized the intellectual, spiritual, pastoral and human development as mainstay of seminary training/activities. Until its issuance, the human aspect of the candidates (crucial as it is) was downplayed in priestly formation.

riences were more or less those they had during their overseas studies. Most of them were sent for further studies soon after their ordinations, and had little or no pastoral ministerial experiences and so could only offer what they have. How can seminaries train future ministers without pastoral studies as a part of their explicit curricula? Can we begin to see reasons for the handicap of the newly ordained in the face of concrete pastoral challenges?

For the priests to be able to minister effectively in the midst of violence, they ought to be prepared for it. For the church leadership to be able to address the issue of domestic violence, the seminary must be a seed ground for such missionary action. As we highlighted in chapter eight, researches indicate that clergy who are not trained for domestic violence are either not ready to handle it or respond to it inappropriately. It is necessary that the Nigerian Church begin the task of accepting domestic violence as an ecclesial mission by its inclusivity in the seminary curriculum. A holistic understanding of the meaning of curriculum is important to enable us appreciate what is been talked about.

The word curriculum comes from the Latin word *currere*, which means to run together. In the educational context, it implies a course to be run. Curriculum in this context includes texts, materials, lesson plans, and specific educational activities by which the school supervises and regulates a course of study. A distinguished curriculum theorist, Elliott Eisner, gives us a broad understanding of curriculum and distinguishes three kinds of curriculum: explicit curriculum, implicit curriculum, and null curriculum. Explicit curriculum refers to the actual content clearly expressed, and consciously and intentionally provided as the teachings of a school. Implicit curriculum has to do with pedagogy, that is, the manner in which teachers teach and interact with students. It also involves the environment that learning takes place. By null curriculum, Eisner refers to the ideas and subjects or areas of study, which are unavailable to the students or refused them.[301] By creating an explicit curriculum, the institution narrows the perspective of students and consequently the spectrum of their thoughts and actions. Students are left to concentrate on what is presented before them for good performances. While explicit curriculum is necessary for the school system, Eisner observes that sometimes, the implicit and null curricula might exert more influence on students than does the explicit curriculum.[302]

To address the issue of curriculum, houses of formation must review their explicit curriculum to accommodate Pastoral Theology and Practical Theological Studies that consider the concrete pastoral situations of ministry. Because domestic violence is a crucial ecclesial and pastoral matter, its study is to become a major theme in the curriculum. It is by having a discussion on the topic that both teachers and students begin to appreciate the relevance of the subject matter to teaching, learning, ministry, and the overall mission of the Nigerian Church. Other contextual pastoral theological issues like Osu Caste System (in Igbo culture) can have the attention they deserve

---

[301] Elliott Eisner, *The Educational Imagination: On the Design and Evolution of School Programs*, second edition, (New York: Macmillan Publishing Co, 1985), 39-40.

[302] Eisner, *The Educational Imagination*, 378.

in theological discourse. The purpose is to equip the priests-to-be with the paraphernalia necessary for their ministry. Exposure to such delicate and challenging pastoral realities is the first step in equipping them for the harsh reality of the ministry else, akin to the biblical converts who were asked if they had received the Holy Spirit,[303] they may reply, "No, we were never even told there was such a thing as this," in the face of such great pastoral need.

The learning environment and pedagogy (implicit curriculum) has to become conducive for adult learning. A recognition that students are adults who have something to present at the table of learning replaces the assumption of teachers that they are neophytes that have come with "blank slates." First, students have experiences and unique insights, which should be midwifed, cherished and made welcome to the learning table. The teachers therefore have to necessarily imbibe a pedagogy that recognizes the agency of students and see themselves and their students as both teachers and learners. Students are practice teachers with one another and with their professors. This operates with the pedagogical assumption that the study of a subject matter is not only done through written texts but also through 'living texts' such as students' wisdom, insights, experiences, cultural backgrounds, worldviews, and critical analysis.[304]

For the training of seminarians in major seminaries in Nigeria, I advocate for a broadening of the seminary curriculum to accommodate a learning and formation that is praxis-oriented and considers

---

[303] Acts 19:2.

[304] Lee, *Transforming Congregations through Community*, 58.

such pastoral and contextual issues as domestic violence. An explicit curriculum that takes care of the ecclesial and pastoral challenges of the local ecclesial, socio-politico-cultural leadership problems and a dialogical pedagogy that disposes both teachers and students for effective learning experience is imperative. As Boyung Lee rightly observes, when the goals of learning, pedagogy, and physical learning environment are compatible with one another, students gain a better understanding of dialogical pedagogy and consequently, good ideas and good experiences, theory and praxis congeal.[305] The result of a good learning experience is confidence and effectiveness in the field of practice. Good, holistic and praxis-oriented learning and formation is what is required to transform the experience of newly ordained priests and provide them the tools for ministry. I also advocate for an ongoing formation of this nature for priests ministering across the dioceses and religious orders. The organization of seminars and workshops to update clergy on the issue of domestic violence and other related pastoral ministerial matters is necessary if the church in Nigeria is to confront adequately the looping pastoral challenges. I argue that the local bishops and the CBCN's ability to train their priests and personnel to minister to victims and victimizers of domestic violence in Nigeria will in no little way help to stem the tide of the phenomenon.

---

[305] Lee, *Transforming Congregations through Community*, 58.

Compassionate Congregational/Parish Curriculum

On leaving the four walls of the seminary, priests find themselves ministering to the people of God. It could be in parishes, schools or other institutions. In whatever case, they find themselves in the midst of men and women, old and young who look up to them for their pastoral and spiritual guidance and nourishment. Arguably, there are in the congregation, victims and survivors of familial violence, perpetrators of the abuse and bystanders. Members as such congregate with their joy and sorrows, knowledge and experiences, stories and biases. The ability of the clergy to exercise their governing, sanctifying and prophetic roles makes a whole lot of difference. An understanding that every opportunity is an occasion to educate in faith enables the church leaders in their ministry to seize every opportunity (*cape diem*) to propagate the faith. Our explanation of curriculum above implies that everything done in church is curriculum. It is about the whole life of the congregation, including the history and reality of a local church as influenced by the larger church and society.[306] In other words, even without uttering a word, the faith community teaches a great deal about her creed and religious practices. When the wealthy are deferred and the less privileged treated with indifference, they teach implicitly that partiality is a way to go. When abused members are blamed and shamed, they imply that abuse is condoned. When preaching on domestic violence is avoided even when the occasion calls for it, the message is

---

[306] Lee, *Transforming Congregations through Community*, 59.

that it is not a problem for the church and that abused members are alone in their pain and struggles.

In the opening words of *Gaudium et Spes* (the Church's Constitution on the Modern World), the Church calls our attention to our common obligation as church community. "The joys and hopes, the sorrows and anxieties of the women and men of this age, especially the poor and those afflicted in any way, are the joys and hopes, the sorrows and anxieties of the followers of Jesus Christ."[307] In the above statement, the fathers of the Second Vatican Council demonstrate the Church's spirit of compassionate sharing and solidarity after the mind of Christ. It represents a challenge to church communities and all the baptized to engage in congregational practices that would help them grow in grace and provide a sustained holistic support to afflicted brethren. It is an injunction and a command for the Church and her individual members to be compassionate and to lend a supportive shoulder for the crushed brethren to lean on. How can the priest minister effectively in a faith community composed of the abused, abusers and bystanders? In what ways can the church community become a welcoming and safe home for all members especially for the most vulnerable? How can the parishes foster a life of communal sharing of joys and sorrows of members in such a way that ensures personal and community flourishing?

"I am because we are, and because we are therefore, I am" is an old African philosophy that bespeaks the people's life of community and interdependence. Put in another way, "one is human because of

---

[307] GS, no. 1.

others, with others and for others." Very much like the Pauline metaphor of the Church as the Body (of Christ) with varied parts all working harmoniously for the good of the whole, the African worldview recognizes the relevance and preciousness of individual members in the community, which defines them more or less. The African communitarian worldview has basis on the understanding of relationships anchored on caring and communal love. Identifying with the Christian faith implies incorporation into a community of persons with individuals belonging to Christ and to one another. From the Pauline theology, we find in this coming together a diversity within unity, with emphasis on communal existence as humankind's fundamental nature as well as the importance of each person's individuality.[308] A Church that values the communal concept of the person, and the Church as the Body of Christ is willing to share the sorrows and joys of members together and at all times.

However, to get a typical Nigerian faith community to start to consider the phenomenon of domestic violence as part of church life or curriculum may not be an easy venture. The strong patriarchal worldview is a large cog in the wheel of transformation. The long and prevalent culture of privacy and shame surrounding the phenomenon makes it difficult to assume a community attention. Yet, domestic violence is not only a matter for public interest but also an issue that requires ecclesial and pastoral response. Much is required in catechesis and education of the faith community in order to package domestic abuse on the ministerial plane. Part of the problem of

---

[308] Lee, *Transforming Congregations through Community*, 32.

194 From Where Shall Come Our Help? The Lament of Abused Persons

Christian religious education is that most believers share the assumption that it is only for children and youth. Lee in *Transforming Congregations through Community* observed that many church members understand Christian education "as the process by which knowledge, tradition, and practices of Christian faith are passed along to the next generations so that children can grow up to be good people."[309] Lee's assessment and observation of her parishioners also reveal that members do not see any connection between Christian education and social transformation. Such identification of religious education with instruction for the purpose of personal growth of young people is true of the Nigerian Church setting.

Against this backdrop, an essential part of the ministerial duties of the clergy is to embark on the catechetical task of broadening their congregations' horizon of salvation and spirituality that includes societal transformation, and the principle of solidarity. The Church religious education will primarily involve and engage the adult parishioners, recognizing the General Catechetical Directory's understanding of adult catechesis as the chief form of catechesis.[310]

An appeal to the African philosophy of communalistic living becomes germinal to provide support and to identify with our suffering brethren. I have reason to believe that there are people who share in the concern for the suffering and dehumanization of victims of

---

[309] Lee, *Transforming Congregations through Community*, 46.

[310] Sacred Congregation for Clergy, *General Catechetical Directory*, no. 20.

domestic violence and the cruelty of the culture. With general education on the social transformational aspect of the gospel message (beginning from the pastoral team to the congregation) and an appeal to our cultural and early church's life of community (Acts 2:44-47; 4:32-35), the church leaders can set up a team of parishioners to engage in ministry that incorporates domestic violence as part of the church curriculum. The mission of the ministry is the emancipation and empowerment of abused persons. The establishment of Ministry of Compassion, Emancipation and Empowerment (MCEE) as an expression of the biblical Christian impulse to be compassionate will lead to a deeper solidarity and greater compassion with victims and survivors, create a safe environment for them, and help to transform the cultural understanding of the phenomenon beginning from the church community.

MCEE membership would comprise of parishioners with the gifts to engage in such dynamic and transformational church ministry. Members will undergo training to equip them with the theological and pedagogical tools necessary for their mission. After a satisfactory period of empowerment, they will in turn be equipped to empower others. MCEE will oversee the parish catechetical and bible studies programs. For legal and training purposes, MCEE can collaborate with FIDA Nigeria, which is an international Non-Governmental Organization (NGO) that advocates for women and children. FIDA (an acronym for the Spanish name "Federacion Internacionale de Abogadas") which translates to "International Federation of Women Lawyers" (IFWL) was formed in 1964 in Nigeria. FIDA Nigeria, like its branches across the world enhances the status of women and children. Its mission is to promote, protect and pre-serve the rights, interests and wellbeing of women and children via the provision of legal framework to ensure their freedom from dis-crimination and violence in the Nigerian society. FIDA Nigeria of-fers free legal representation for indigent women and children, ad-vocacy, and policy campaigns, education and training, mediation and counseling services, and publication of information services.[311] Church communities are to tap into FIDA's education and training services for MCEE and congregation, and their advocacy, media-tion, counseling, and publication services in providing support to domestic violence victims and survivors. This partnership is essen-tial and will bolster the victim parishioners' sense of security and provide them legal support.

From the church angle, MCEE can liaise with the diocesan Jus-tice Development and Peace Commission (JDPC). The JDPC is an organ of the Catholic Church that is concerned with matters of jus-tice and humanitarian support to church members and communi-ties.[312] The commission has the task of examining issues connected with justice with the aim of awakening believers to greater under-standing of justice issues and awareness of their roles as well as their responsibility in the spheres of justice, the development of people,

---

[311] "We Are Experienced Female Lawyers," FIDA Nigeria, accessed November 21, 2021, www.fida.org.ng.

[312] Most dioceses in Nigeria have the JDPC department at the diocesan level and some equally have established it at the parishes.

human advancement, peace and human rights.[313] This collaboration is necessary because of the broader ecclesial connection and the socio-economic support involved. Church communities could obtain from JDPC material support for economically abused members. It may be necessary to partner with JDPC to build shelters for abused women and children. This facility would foster the security and empowerment of domestic violence victims in a society that scarcely has such resources.

The assumption is that the parish community, through the MCEE's core mission, shall become a place of life, love and hope, amidst the ineffectiveness of state and society to guarantee safety and human flourishing of the most vulnerable citizens. The aim is to make the faith community a place where victims of domestic violence would be safe to tell their stories and be believed, and have their experiences validated. It would be a strong support system to help them cope with their suffering and pain. MCEE shall operate under the leadership of a committee made up of committed parishioners and professionals like attorneys, doctors and Social Workers. MCEE will ensure that sexual and domestic violence become topics taught in all church education programs including but not limited to parish bible study, Youth and Adult catechism classes and pre-marriage courses. While the MCEE members partner with the priest in the various church faith education curriculum, the priest primar-

---

[313] "History – Justice Development & Peace Commission," Justice Development and Peace Commission Ibadan, accessed November 21, 2021, www.jdpcibadan.org.

ily uses the pulpit as a veritable platform to demonstrate his commitment to resistance to the dominate narrative of domestic violence, transformation, hope and healing to victims and survivors of abuse. With the high level of familial violence in the country, we have the assumption that a praxis ministry can help the Nigerian women and children concretely gain a sense of their human dignity and rights, and enjoy the support of a system that guarantees their safety and empowerment.

Praxis-oriented Ministry

Throughout this book, we argue that domestic violence is an ecclesial and existential matter that requires the church's attention and intervention. If this is true, (and certainly, it is) then it requires church leadership to take appropriate theological and pastoral steps in response. We submit that in response to the prevalent phenomenon, a praxis-oriented ministerial approach is required and will engender resourcefulness and transformation. For Groome, who advocates a praxis pastoral ministry,[314] the Christian ministry is an inclusive enterprise where all has the task to witness to the reign of God, and as a community provide personal and social services for the welfare of all and good of God's creation. A praxis-oriented pastoral ministry is a Christian ministry where people congregate into

---

[314] Thomas Groome's Shared Christian Praxis is both an educational and pastoral tool. The Praxis is active, reflective, creative and thus transformational. My idea of praxis-oriented ministry is influenced by Groome's praxis approach to religious education and ministry.

partnership and community. It is a ministerial environment where the preciousness and value of members are rooted in the common priesthood of the faithful accorded all by baptism. A praxis-based ministry is devoted to paying attention to the existential issues in the lives of people, engaging such challenges and thus ministering to people's pertinent needs. Here people's stories and experiences are taken seriously. It means empowering people to take on the issues and needs of their lives and to respond to them together out of Christian faith.[315]

Understanding domestic violence and its prevalence in Nigeria as an ecclesial and pastoral issue, its impact in the lives of its victims becomes an "ecclesial action" which church leaders bring up in ministry. This awareness generates an attitude that leads to an engagement with the phenomenon and identification with its victims with the intent to end the abuse and to foster the emancipation and human flourishing of its victims. The ability of the religious leaders to name the evil and do ministry in such a way that invites congregants to express their agency and stories is itself empowering.

The way we talk about domestic violence in a church setting is important. Maintaining the old stereotype of patriarchy and subjugation of women is harmful to victims and to the entire congregation. It is unhelpful when the element of "thoughtfulness" is lacking in the conversation. The component of remembering and critically reflecting on the socio-cultural context that breeds violence and stifle human dignity and rights of some members of the community or

---

[315] Groome, *Sharing Faith*, 333.

society is important. This critical consciousness of the historical reality or what Freire calls *conscientization* becomes a means by which persons, through a true praxis, abandon the status of objects, take up the status of subjects, and thus are in a position to see what they ought to see and hear what they ought to hear.[316] Thus, people could question their assumptions about violence as victims and as perpetrators and perchance be able to see the heinousness of its internalization (by victims) and its perpetration (by victimizers). In preaching and religious education, religious leaders recognize their obligation to speak the truth about domestic violence; are able to stimulate critical and creative reflection to assist church members (calling all in the pews, victims, perpetrators and bystanders) come to grasp and discern what is "going on" in their lives.[317] Thus, congregants come to greater grasp regarding the impact or consequences of the phenomenon in their lives, family, community and society.

The Church has rich and profound resources at her disposal to support and promote the wellbeing of the community. The praxis as an educational and ministerial tool "reminds that Christian ministers are to embody in deed and make accessible in word and sacraments the reality of God's saving presence and intentions of fullness of life for all humankind, with special preference for people whose life and wellbeing is most denied."[318] Ministry is not to serve the purpose of soothing the dives. Preaching, pastoral counseling, and every

---

[316] Freire, *Pedagogy*, 160.

[317] Groome, *Will There Be Faith*, 315.

[318] Groome, *Sharing Faith*, 333-334.

other ministry are to present the scripture and church teaching in a manner that reflects the will of God for humanity. Like Jesus, the good news is to be preached to the afflicted (Luke 4: 18), the good news of their liberation, of the restoration of their wounded body and healing to their crushed spirit.

Genuine ministry maintains openness to the direction and prompting of the Spirit. Openness to the Spirit leads us to listen to one another and to appreciate one another in a giving and receiving encounter. The minister, through a praxis lens is attentive to and open to receive from others to whom and with whom they minister. In the context of pastoral counseling, the minister listens to the abused person's story, believes them and validates their story rather than being judgmental. The relationship between the minister and their abused parishioner is that of subject-agents-in-relationship; the congregant is no passive recipient of ministry but a recipient of a human service who deserves their dignity.

Ultimately, ministry to and with people with pastoral needs is not such that people remain where they were; it is not simply about meeting the needs of the situation but rather involves improving the situation. The minister is poised to transform the status quo and guide the community to this end. The goal of ministering to victims of domestic violence is their emancipation and human flourishing. Through the lens of Groome's Shared Christian Praxis, the emphasis is the

empowerment of people as agent-subjects, humanly and in faith – whatever their faith may be – that people may come to act and be actors in humanizing and faith-filled ways...existentially, of course, there can be situations where Christian ministry does well to alleviate immediate human need and suffering. However, it is always to be suffused as well with intent to change the situation, to help people to help themselves and others."[319]

The people, as agent-subjects, are part of the project, called, as they are, to take certain decisions and make some responses.

An effective application and implementation of a praxis-oriented ministry in a Nigerian pastoral context will certainly face two huge challenges. One is the ability of the clergy to accept the "ground level" nature of the praxis, and the other is for the parishioners to "unlearn" the interiorized mentality of the dominant narrative. First, the clergy enjoy the power and authority they have and may perceive the praxis ministry as a threat to their privileged position. A praxis ministry involves developing a subject-subject relationship with others, and having a participatory and partnership model of ministry. It reaches out to where the people are, at the ground level. It requires the clergy to engage in critique of the status quo and the readiness to transform the dominant narrative. This may be challenging. Second, in chapter two, we examined how their men counterparts have socialized Nigerian women and children to accept the narrative of their subjection and dominance. The process of unlearning this narrative may be laborious and may impact the receptivity and effectiveness of a praxis approach.

---

[319] Groome, *Sharing Faith*, 334.

In an appraisal of the Shared Christian Praxis, Remigius Nwabichie wagers that it is a viable alternative approach to religious education in Nigeria. Making a constructive critique of the religious education model of the early Irish missionaries to Nigeria, he argues strongly for the appropriation of the shared praxis for the Igbo Nigeria educational and pastoral institutions. He sees the Igbo sense of community as a seed ground.[320] (We shall detail on this Igbo cultural value in the next chapter). Nwabichie, however, failed to raise the question of power differential in contemporary Igbo (Nigeria) society especially in the church context. I submit that the implementation of shared praxis in the Nigerian ministerial context is feasible, though will require a considerable time and adaptation.[321]

Our ultimate goal is to begin to close the gap between the lack of resources and support for many victims of domestic violence and their need for emancipation and human flourishing in pastoral ministry in the Nigerian context. Engagement in ministry and ministerial programs that focus on emotional, legal, and spiritual support for victims of domestic violence in Nigeria based on the theological notion of compassion as a biblical imperative and on a praxis approach is crucial. How to engage in such style of ministry and the specific ministries will be the task of the following chapters.

---

[320] Remigius Nwabichie, *A Philosophy for the Christian Education of the Igbo of the Southeastern Nigeria: Thomas Groome's Shared Praxis Approach* (PhD diss., Fordham University, 2018), 248-49.

[321] In the next chapter, we shall apply shared praxis not only in preaching and pastoral counseling, as did Thomas Groome but also adapt it to Women Support Group for abused women.

CHAPTER TWELVE

COMPASSION-PRAXIS PREACHING

Breaking the Silence from the Pulpit

"Although there are many ways to break the silence in our churches, the most central and pivotal place of all is from the pulpit. Nowhere else can we so clearly communicate that the church does not turn its back on victims and survivors of abuse."[322] The above assertion of John McClure underscores the importance of the "Liturgy of the Word" in congregational worship. What is preached is supposedly the Word of God, and people look forward to God's promise to them and what God is calling them to do with their lives. Congregants gather to be fed with the Word of God, which is spiritual food for their nourishment and transformation. The sermon therefore, becomes a powerful handy tool of the Church in response to domestic violence. Preaching can serve both to transform the structure that is responsible for the suffering and to empower the lives of the victims of suffering. Barbara Patterson strongly believes that preaching can be an activist and transformative response by the church to violence against women. In order for this to happen, Patterson suggests that preachers must learn to approach preaching as part of a daily Christian practice of resisting violence. This practice encourages us to ask some difficult questions about abuse, scripture,

---

[322] John McClure, "Preaching about Sexual and Domestic Violence," 111.

God, and ourselves. Such questions include, what difference will our sermons make for these women, our parishes, God, and ourselves? Will our homilies engender understanding, compassion, and active justice?[323] These crucial questions should inform any transformational, compassionate preaching.

When the priest stands on the pulpit to preach a homily, he is aware that he ministers in a church that operates on a lectionary-based liturgy. This fundamentally regulates his homily themes. While it is possible to engage in preaching a nonviolent theology, which can occur not only in thematic violence sermons but also in all sermons,[324] the best bet would be to look for opportunities to speak about domestic violence as they arise. A preaching on domestic violence could occur on Feast of Holy Family, Mother's Day, Father's Day, Catholic Women Organization (CWO) monthly mass/devotion, liturgies that the readings allude to it, and situational contexts (preaching) like weddings, wedding anniversaries and funerals.

Preaching in a context with dense cases of domestic violence, the priest becomes conscious of the category of people that form his congregation. Unarguably in the assembly, there are victims and survivors of familial abuse, perpetrators, and bystanders. A compassionate preaching provides comfort and protection to the afflicted,

---

[323] Barbara Patterson, "Preaching as Nonviolent Resistance" in in *Telling the Truth: Preaching about Sexual and Domestic Violence,* ed. John McClure and Nancy Ramsay (Cleveland, OH: United Church Press, 1998), 99.

[324] McClure, "Preaching about Sexual and Domestic Violence," 113.

brings perpetrators to consciousness of their guilt, and to bystanders, the sense of responsibility.

On delivering a compassion-praxis sermon on domestic violence, the preacher sets the following goals: First, to break the silence that has prevailed for a longtime on the phenomenon, to unveil the privacy and secrecy that surrounds it, and to challenge individual and systemic violence. Second, to proclaim a word of hospitality, resistance, and hope to victims and survivors. Third, to put across a message that the church will no longer be a place of cheap grace for violence offenders. Finally, to invite the parish community to examine how it might become a safe place as well as a force for resistance, compassion and empowerment as it concerns domestic violence.[325]

The aim is to create the awareness that domestic violence is evil and that as a church we have a moral obligation to speak to it and against it; we are all involved and must together address it. The goal is to make the liturgy and the worshipping community a holding environment for the abused persons' pain and suffering. Vulnerable parishioners need to know that the sanctuary is a safe place where members can hold their kind of pain and affliction. The assurance of God's love for them offers them hope and healing.

Every anonymous victim of violence who worships should hear over and over again about the intimate, delicious kindness and goodness of God. Every woman trying to live a human life when her image of herself is as a worthless worm should hear about

---

[325] McClure, "Preaching about Sexual and Domestic Violence," 111.

the beauty of her soul, made by God, loved for its own unique and irreplaceable strength and loveliness.[326]

A sermon that gives hope to abused women can in effect be empowering and foster healing. There is power in the word, enormous and transformational power indeed.

Unfortunately, we ministers have often deceived perpetrators of abuse by offering them the cheap grace of forgiveness. Some of us play down on the harm done by violence and only erroneously harp on the need for forgiveness that rightly speaking is premature at the time. The truth has to be told with some clarity about the heinousness of abuse and how forgiveness is earned in the face of such human atrocity. Forgiveness is not the first word in a case of abuse; repentance and restitution precede it if it is to feature in the first place. While perpetrators can obtain absolution through the means of the sacrament of reconciliation, they must be reminded of accountability for their ungodly actions and behaviors. Habitual abusers must be encouraged to seek counseling for transformation. The ultimate aim is to change the dominant narrative of men's subjugation of women. It is about establishing a preferred narrative as a community, which will promote the human flourishing of all and sundry. Together, in compassion, we can make the parish a holding environment, a safe place for all members especially for the most vulnerable.

---

[326] Farley, "Evil, Violence, and the Practice of Theodicy," 17.

For the homily to do justice to the above goals, we recommend that it features the following elements:

Story - Naming the reality of domestic violence is crucial and this can be done effectively by telling a story of abuse. This is done in such a way that the story reflects the theme of the homily – domestic violence- and what Groome calls "sermon sources,"[327] namely, the existential lives and circumstances of the people, the historical context of the community/society, the preacher's life/ministerial experience, and the scripture readings of the day. The story serves to lead congregants to recognize what is going on in their lives regarding the theme. They eventually come to identify themselves in the story as perpetrators, bystanders or victims as it relates to the forms of domestic violence. Through self-reflective questions, they are assisted to name what is going on or what they need to name. The purpose is for congregants to recognize the preaching as something that pertains to their lives. Each participant should be able to say, "This preaching resonates with me/my life."

Critical reflection: At this point, the homily turns into a critical reflection that engages congregants. The minister leads the assembly to consider the memories, history, consequences of the phenomenon on personal, ecclesial and social dimensions. An analysis of the situation for people's consideration may be necessary. How do we justify a man battering his wife and children? Is there anything that

---

[327] Groome, *Sharing Faith*, 375.

makes men more human than women? Why are we, the church, unable to respond to the needs of our vulnerable members? How can we make the church a safe place for all?

Exegesis of Scripture readings: Attention now goes to the scripture readings of the day. The minister engages on a hermeneutic of the assigned readings in such a way that it ultimately has a practical bearing in people's lives and context. Talking about the manner in which a preacher does exegesis in a conversational style, McClure observes: "In this conversation, as the text is interpreted, he gives voice to the interpretation of many who have not been heard but who are in the congregation: the abused, abusers, bystanders, social workers, families, friends and more."[328] Scripture is God's word of promise to his people and the abused ought to hear message/words of good news to the afflicted, liberty to captives, sight to the blind, freedom for the oppressed and God's time of favor.[329] Same Scripture contains word of challenge to bear responsibility for our actions. Offenders and bystanders should be greeted with words that make them do a *mea culpa* and to act subsequently in a responsible fashion.

Appropriation: Hermeneutics that reflects practical wisdom engages people and necessarily leads them into personal appropriation. The people are encouraged to consider what meaning the passage and

---

[328] McClure, "Preaching about Sexual and Domestic Violence," 117.
[329] Lk 4: 18.

message has for their lives. The passage may contain "appropriatea-ble" messages; the minister may also highlight the challenge that the message poses to them. It may be accountability and a new attitude to power for perpetrators, courage and sense of responsibility for bystanders, and hope for victims and survivors.

Decision-making: There is an invitation to participants for them to make decisions about the present praxis. The preacher poses ques-tions that invite decisions and responses from them. What will you ask God to help you do to make your home safe? What will you try to change in your life/relationship with your spouse and children? Suggesting possible decisions for people's consideration is encour-aged.

A homily that reflects the above elements puts some aspect of the congregants' present historical reality in dialogue with some as-pect of the Scripture message. This is with the hope that people are empowered to see the import of the Christian faith in their lives and spurred with the commitment to live it out. For Groome and McClure, a good homily has to be conversational. Homily from the Latin word *homilein* means to have a conversation. Homily has to be conversational or dialogical in order to engage the congregation. The preacher has to preach not at the congregation but with them. Even when only the preacher speaks (as is usually the case), the preaching is dialogical if it engages people and leads them to active recognition, imagination, remembering, reasoning, judgment, dis-cernment and decision about what Scriptures mean for their present lives and what God is calling them to do in their lives. The purpose is to lead parishioners to experience radical changes in their worldviews and theology and to transform the parish community's self-understanding and commitment to the Christian message and witnessing. Such environment thus becomes safe and therapeutic for the vulnerable members and for the larger society.

CHAPTER THIRTEEN

PASTORAL COUNSELING
AND SUPPORT FOR VICTIMS OF DOMESTIC VIOLENCE

Meeting Victim's Pastoral Counseling Needs

As indicated in chapter five from the survey of Okemgbo, Omideyi and Odimegwu, abused women in Nigeria do turn to significant persons in their lives including religious leaders as their first resource for help in the event of domestic violence. This reality, coupled with the welcoming and safe environment created by the church parish curriculum including faith education and preaching, gives reason to believe that abused women and children parishioners will be more disposed to access pastoral counseling opportunities. Following Howard Clinebell's functions of pastoral care and counseling,[330] Groome articulates the following pastoral counseling goals:

to *heal* people in their brokenness from hurts of life and from personality disorders; to *sustain* people to live faithfully in life's struggles and to support them in times of crisis (death, divorce, illness, etc,); to offer *guidance* in times of confusion and decision making; to *reconcile* people with themselves, others, and God

---

[330] Howard Clinebell, *Basic Types of Pastoral Care and Counseling: Resources for the Ministry of Healing and Growth*, 3rd ed. (Nashville, TN: Abingdon Press, 2011), 40-41.

and to assure them of God's never-ending mercy; to offer *nurture* and companionship in people's spiritual journey.[331]

Victims and survivors of marital violence will require pastoral counseling to help them on their healing trajectory, and to assist them make decisions about possible emancipatory options. It also guides them in the midst of their struggles and challenges, to reconcile with themselves in the midst of self-guilt and low self-esteem, and to nurture their relationship with God and the church in the face of unwarranted pain and suffering. In all, pastoral counseling provides abused persons empowerment and an opportunity to inform, form, and transform them in Christian identity.

While some parishioners may come up to share their stories of abuse and seek pastoral assistance, the priest will have to be on the look out to observe compassionately, signs of abuse on others. Suggesting on pastoral response of clergypersons to the abused congregants, Cooper-White enjoins ministers to be able to observe signs of abuse among their parishioners. Common indicators of abuse, according to her, include women who exhibit hypervigilance or startle response, those who appear to have more bruises and injuries than expected, and those with anxiety or anxiety-related health issues like ulcers and headache.[332] To make these observations and to get the desired results, the expectation is that the clergy take time to know

---

[331] Groome, *Sharing Faith,* 411.

[332] Cooper-White, *The Cry of Tamar,* 144.

their parishioners, be pastorally observant, and develop a relationship of trust with their members.

Cooper-White further recommends that when the environment is safe and abuse is suspected, questions could be asked to inquire if the parishioner is a victim of domestic violence. It is no doubt that such bold step will in many cases break the silence and initiate parishioner marital violence victims' journey toward emancipation, justice and healing. In pastoral counseling, the pastoral needs of such parishioners are ministered to. Pastoral counseling can take a group or one-on-one context. The priest is encouraged to embark on the latter; it will offer individual counselees a safe space given the delicacy of familial violence. A compassion-praxis pastoral counseling session will have the following moments:

Counseling relationship: literature on counseling speak about the importance of establishing a good and positive counseling relationship between the counselor and the counselee. It behooves the counselor to create this positive emotional environment. This is necessary to win the counselee's trust. Clergy ability to handle victims' matters confidentially in all dimensions of pastoral ministry and maintaining healthy boundaries, the attention given to counselees, and clergy general demeanor are crucial in establishing a relationship of trust with parishioners who make themselves available for pastoral counseling. This amounts to a subject-to-subject relationship that recognizes the agency of the counselee, "encouraging an environment of hospitality and respect, trust and openness, one in which the counselee feels safe and at home enough to take the risk of honest conversation."[333]

Validation of victim's story: behind every face, there is a story. The victim has a unique story. To disbelieve her story is to send her back into oblivious silence. It is important to offer supportive listening attention, and empathic and non-anxious presence. To trust her and to validate her story is comforting and ensures her trust and confidence in the minister. The priest lets her know that she is not alone and assure her of his support in her struggle.

Addressing victim's sense of guilt: as observed in chapters one and two, the Nigerian context is such that women have been socialized to believe that they are the cause of their abuse and that men have the right to batter them in certain cases. A good counseling step will be to make them realize that violence against them is never their fault. The priest counselor ought to let her know that she is a crime victim and the responsibility of the crime lies not on her but on her abuser. The problem lies on our culture and system that unfortunately marginalizes womenfolk to men's undue advantage.

Prioritizing victim's safety: abused women often get into trouble with their abusive partners when the abusers become aware of any case of reporting of their abusive relationship to an "outsider." Telling others their abusive stories is breaking the abuser's "isolation rules" and may incur his wrath. The safety of the counselee is therefore a matter of priority to the priest counselor. The minister should

---

[333] Groome, *Sharing Faith*, 420.

honor "her intuition at all times about what is safe for her, and remember to raise the issue of safety periodically even if she does not."[334] This requires the priest to keep their conversation confidential and away from her abuser and notifying her of the need to report to security agencies when threat to her life becomes acute.

Respecting counselee's self-determination right: in pastoral counseling, the counselee usually takes the lead; the pastoral counselor only follows and supports her actions. Except for imminent and serious danger cases, when there may be need for security, the victim must take the decisions and actions. About respecting victim's right of self-determination, Cooper-White offers the following suggestions to pastors and pastoral caregivers: "Do not press her into action, but respect her process and her sense of what is safe. Give her options and resources, but do not insist."[335] The pastoral counselor, ought to be aware therefore, that the recognition of the self-determination of a victim of abuse is a recognition of their agency and a sure way of empowering them. This includes the issue of forgiveness. It is not the priest counselor's duty to compel her to forgive her abuser or to remain in a relationship. A non-anxious presence, a non-judgmental stance, and the assurance of consistent emotional and spiritual support are imperative.

Assurance of God's love: as indicated in chapter three, some abused persons experience trouble in relating with God and the church. It is hard for some to reconcile a loving and caring God with

---

[334] Cooper-White, *The Cry of Tamar*, 145.

[335] Cooper-White, *The Cry of Tamar*, 146.

the suffering and pain they experience. It becomes important to let them know that the suffering is not God's plan for them. They are loved by God and do not in any way deserve to be abused. God wills human flourishing and abundant life for them. God identifies with us in our suffering and indeed suffers with us as the kenosis reveals.

Referral and other resources: The priest becomes aware that as a pastoral care provider his support to victims and survivors of domestic violence is limited. Victims may require expertise help and resources that are beyond the priest's competence. He should therefore be ready to make referrals to therapists and for other logistical supports when necessary. Other specialized assistance may include financial, medical and legal aids that the counselee may need on her emancipation and healing trajectory. FIDA and JDPC are resourceful agencies to which abused persons may be referred. The priest should encourage counselees to join the Women Support Group (WSG), which is a group of victims and survivors of domestic violence for the purpose of empowering and supporting one another. The activities of WSG will be discussed below.

Through the counseling sessions, the counselor ought to assist abused persons to uncover suppressed myths, forgotten memories, neglected images, and socialized assumptions around domestic violence that have so negatively impacted their self-image and emancipation. The aim is to see the heinousness of the dominant narrative and to seek for a new and preferred narrative. According to Groome, the healing and emancipatory potential of pastoral counseling depends largely on the "un-covering" and "dis-covering" element of it.[336] "Un-covering" the evil of domestic violence and "dis-covering" options of seeing things differently, and providing alternative worldviews give abused persons enormous hope and strength on the healing and emancipation trajectory.

Women Support Group

The gathering of victims and survivors of domestic violence will constitute a powerful solidarity and a veritable avenue for their healing and empowerment. Through the agency of MCEE, pastoral counseling and preaching, abused women will be encouraged to gather for group support. Individual women who face abuse in their homes and workplaces have unique stories to tell concerning the forms, severity, and frequency of violence confronting them. The establishment of Women Support Group (WSG) where victims and survivors of abuse tell their stories becomes one of the means through which these vulnerable members of the church community can congregate for mutual support with the aim of fostering healing and transformation. We imagine that the constitution of a separate group of abused women might be slimly possible under the current Nigerian environment. This is though possible within a socio-politico-religious context that contains women of same interest and goal, which may cut across faith affiliations. For faith communities or parishes, we suggest that Christian women make WSG a part of their usual group gathering. This can be appreciated given the fact that,

---

[336] Groome, *Sharing Faith*, 421.

as we aforesaid, every woman is likely to experience domestic violence at one point or another in her life. Again, part of the women groups' agenda is the welfare of members. What welfare could rank higher than the end or mitigation of violence against womenfolk?

MCEE can thus liaise with the faith community's Catholic Women Organization (CWO) and National Confraternity of Christian Mothers (NCCM).[337] The women group of the various sodalities in the parish can also appropriate the WSG agenda to their regular program. The aim is to break the silence on the violence against women and to support one another in a fight that involves them all as women.

In the gathering of the women, the sharing of stories is highly encouraged. This is because of the terrific power of storytelling. In *Soul Stories*, Anne Wimberly opines that,

> [S]tories reveal the very lives persons live and lives for which they hope. Stories reveal persons' yearning for God's liberating presence and activity in their lives. And they reveal persons' yearning for meaning and purpose in life. Stories also reveal God's concrete presence and action in persons' lives and persons' responses to God."[338]

---

[337] A couple of provinces or regions in Nigeria have other Christian Women groups besides the CWO like the NCCM in Lagos and Abuja archdioceses/provinces. Whatever the name or designation, we advocate for incorporation of the WSG into their group life and operation.

[338] Anne Wimberly, *Soul Stories: African American Christian Education* (Nashville, TN: Abingdon Press, 1994), 38.

The meeting of the group will be such that members' personal stories and experiences are put in parallel with the Christian Story and Vision.

The group meets weekly or biweekly at a time convenient for all participants and the meeting will begin with welcoming of members by the facilitator[339] and an opening prayer. There is a choice of song that expresses emancipation and God's love for the oppressed (like the popular song *Amazing Grace* by John Newton). Any member can take the opening prayer as the spirit directs; the prayer will reflect the hopes and aspirations of members in God who is always faithful. The facilitator will anchor the group activities through the following six phases:

Phase one: Telling an abuse story. The story told by the facilitator serves as a lens through which the theme of domestic violence becomes the focus of the activity. Beginning with a concrete story that reflects the everyday life events of the people bespeaks the importance of their context and experiences. According to Wimberly, our stories are the agenda we bring to our study of Christian faith story and it is crucial that we disclose this agenda in order to let our own stories be formed and informed by the Christian faith story,[340] even as the Christian story is in turn challenged and enhanced by them. Participants are invited to identify with the story. This can be done by asking the following or similar questions: In what ways are

---

[339] The facilitator can be a survivor or a member of MCEE. It is not a permanent status but a position that is rotatory once members are able to anchor the group gathering.

[340] Wimberly, *Soul Stories*, 40.

the story your story? Do you have difficulty relating to the story, and if so why? In what ways do you justify the action of the male partner? What did the story evoke in you? The purpose of the story and the activity or questions arising from the story is to bring to the consciousness of participants what is going on in their lives and relationships regarding the abuse of their dignity and rights. Here the facilitator is helping them to recognize the reality of what is been talked about in their lives and context.

Phase two: Moving next will be a social analysis of domestic violence in the homes, churches and society. This phase considers how the cultural context breeds abuse of women by making women subordinates of men, the understanding of marriage as an institution where women always obey their husbands even when they are wrong, the doctrine of forgiveness, and the complacence of both civil and ecclesial authorities in all of this. Participants will critically reflect on and how women have come to be socialized to internalize and accept the culture of abuse of their human dignity and rights. The following questions are relevance here: What gives the men the impetus to batter their wives? Do women in any way deserve battery? Does your marriage and family reflect your expectation of marriage and family, and if not, what is your ideal of the institutions? How have we come to internalize abuse from men as the norm? The purpose of the critical questioning and analysis of the context is to lead participants to recognize that something is wrong with the dominant narrative of violence against women and to begin to think about preferred or alternative narrative.

Phase three: One of the participants will read a passage of the bible. As we observed in chapter five, men have often used Scripture as a tool in the oppression of women. Nicole Simpson, from a feminist viewpoint observes that, Scripture has been weaponized to keep women in a second-class position in church and society and so, standing alone, it is not necessarily presented as the ideal instrument for use in the healing and empowerment of abused women. She however opines that same Scripture can be used to confront the issue with liberating and empowering reading and hermeneutics of biblical texts that challenge sexual bias.[341] I believe with Simpson that a different interpretation of Scripture can reveal to us a place in the same Scriptures, which historically have served a detrimental purpose, to promote healing, wholeness and transformation of women.

In the use of Scripture, the group will make choice of passages of the Old and New Testaments that tell about freedom and counter freedom stories as well as salvation stories. Laments especially as contained in the book of Psalms will make good choices. The stories of abused women like Tamar the wife of Er (Gen 38), Hagar the Egyptian slave girl (Gen 16), Tamar daughter of David (2 Sam 13), and the woman caught in adultery (Jn 8: 1-11) or similar stories could be read. The reading and discussion on the biblical texts is in such a way that it has a practical bearing in the lives and circumstances of participants, and invites them to discern for themselves

---

[341] Nicole Simpson, "Life after Sexual Trauma and Incarceration: A Restoration model for wholeness for Women who suffered Sexual Violence" (DMin Thesis, Boston University, 2020), 32.

the meaning for their lives. Depending on the number of participants, people may be requested to be in small groups to share reflec-
tions on the reading. The activity is such that participants feel free
and express their feeling as they reflect on the passage in the light of
their life experiences. They may express anger on texts of counter
freedom and injustice, peace and contentment on freedom texts.
They should also be able to ask questions about the text as well as
give insights as they come to them about the text.

Phase four: After reading and analyzing the biblical passage, participants begin to consider what meaning the passage has for them
as abused persons. The participants are able to identify and discern
the implications of the scriptural reading in the concreteness of their
lives. The step toward emancipation, justice, healing and transformation has its own challenges. It requires the virtue of courage. The
biblical text and the group support can serve to gain the needed
courage and to appropriate the wisdom of Scripture. Such questions
as what they think the passage requires of them is important. Specifically, they may have to consider the following questions: How does
the scripture passage speak to you? What do you imagine is the will
of God for you? Do you suppose that God plans liberation or cap-
tivity for you?

Phase five: It is important that participants come to a moment in
the group sharing when each person has to make a decision about
her life and attitude to violence against her as informed by the day's
activity. The decisions and responses may range from breaking the
silence to taking legal actions regarding her abusive relationship.
The following or similar questions may be proposed. What will you

ask God to help you do to live a flourishing life? What will you ask God to help you to overcome your abusive relationship? How do you think you can contribute to the fight against sexual violence and domestic violence in our community and society? The facilitator may also suggest possible decisions for the consideration of participants. Secular and biblical heroines may be presented to them as a model of courage and faith-filled response. From the story of Tamar in 2 Samuel 13, participants may be encouraged to let their voice be heard in the midst of violence than internalize it or take it as a norm. Tamar the wife of Er's ability to seize the slim opportunity she had to protest against her father-in-law's injustice could serve them as an exemplar. Deborah, Judith and Esther are biblical heroines that could bolster abused women's courage to attain emancipation and transformation.

Phase six: Prayer/ritual is a powerful violence resistance strategy. Laments are crucial here. (*The Power of Lament* is a postscript to this book). Participants may read lament psalm in turn by verses meditatively involving everyone present. Rituals could include praying for repentance of perpetrators of domestic violence, for the abolition of the culture of violence against women and children and for government and her agencies who make decisions that affect the safety and rights of women. According to Traci West, the frequent holding of ritual, which includes naming, and ritually denouncing violence is a veritable pastoral response to domestic violence.[342] I have put in

---

[342] Traci West, "Sustaining an Ethic of Resistance against Domestic Violence in Black Faith-Based Communities" in *Domestic Violence at the*

the appendix a prayer/ritual that can be of use for this session of the Women Support Group.

Finally, the WSG can engage in other activities to support one another and to promote resistance against domestic violence. These may include outreach programs and retreats. I expect that members of the group will include some women who have surmounted the phenomenon of marital violence in their life and are ready to help other women with their experiences. Looking up to such women, others struggling with their abusive relationships will draw hope, strength and inspiration. Having more and more women find resources from the ecclesial community to deal with their abusive relationships and experience healing and human flourishing will have gone a long way to fill the yawning gap between the high prevalence of domestic violence in the Nigerian society and its mitigation. This book would have then achieved its transformative objective.

Margins, ed. Natalie Sokoloff (New Jersey: Rutgers University Press, 2005), 343.

FINAL THOUGHTS

The primary objective of this publication was to provide a framework that Nigerian church communities could utilize to address the prevalent domestic violence in homes, churches, workplaces and society. This book has the expectation of transforming the structure that is responsible for domestic violence as well as fostering healing and empowering the lives of victims and survivors of domestic violence, beginning with the church. It is common knowledge that change is difficult and people hardly take the risk. In assent with Robert Quinn, Richard Osmer rightly observes, "Leading deep change is costly and risky. Leaders must carry out the "internal work" of discerning their own core values, as well as the "inner voice" of the organization they are leading."[343] Abused women and children look forward to church communities and leaders who are ready and willing to lend them a supporting hand in their struggle to attain healing and wholeness and to provide them with the resources they need.

When asked how to tackle the problem of poverty in the world, Theresa of Calcutta responded that one has to begin by feeding the poor person nearest to them. Like poverty, domestic violence is ravaging our world. Every concerned person or institution has to begin from somewhere. The mantra, 'if you see something, say something' is crucial and applicable here. Beyond talking, we have to be ready to walk the talk. The sociocultural reality of the Nigerian populace

---

[343] Richard Osmer, *Practical Theology: An Introduction* (Grand Rapids, MI: Wm. B. Eerdmans Publishing Co., 2008), 177-78.

is one of high rate of abuse of women and children and it can only take Nigerians, victims, victimizers and bystanders in time and place to address this big elephant in the room. While there are scanty research works done on the subject matter of domestic violence in Nigeria, there is scarcely any theological discourse on this prevalent phenomenon in the country. The awareness of the heinousness of the evil needs to be created; political and ecclesial leadership ought to be challenged; the dominant narrative of male dominance and subjugation of women has to be transformed. This task requires theological enterprise.

Domestic violence involves suffering; human suffering is particularly relevant to the field of pastoral theology. Many issues that pastoral theology deal with concern the human body: the sick body, the dying body, the addicted body, the depressed body, the abused body. The matter of embodied beauty, suffering, pain and redemption, and how they are enabled or hindered by social context, is focal to pastoral theology.[344] Theology is about theory and practice; theology is life. We have demonstrated that domestic violence is an ecclesial and theological issue. A discourse on the phenomenon of domestic violence involves a conversation on the subject matter as well as practical pastoral steps to address the problem. Novel as they may be, we have, in the course of this work, outlined several pastoral responses to the problem of domestic violence in Nigeria. While the issue is complex and involves all agents of socialization, the church

---

[344] Susan Dunlap, *Caring Cultures: How Congregations respond to the Sick* (Waco, TX: Baylor University Press, 2009), 8.

as a moral authority has a crucial role to play to curb the impact of this structural evil in the Nigerian society.

Domestic violence, as a matter of fact, lead us to realize that sometimes it is hard to keep spirituality and culture/politics apart. It challenges ministers to acknowledge and undertake the missionary task of social transformation. Barbara Patterson underscores that the transformative role of preachers puts ministers of the word on an edge.

> As preachers resisting violence against women, we are putting our bodies, minds, and souls on the line with women abused, raped, and beaten. These women also, in various states and ways, participate in Christ's body. We are bound to one another, and so we preach about their reality and what we know and experience.[345]

Pastoral response to domestic violence though a risky enterprise, it is worth the risk for it is part of our calling as ministers and as God's children. It involves leading a "deep change." Little wonder it is risky and expensive. However, it unites us to the sufferers and unites us to the body of Christ and ultimately to Christ who suffered for us and identifies with our abused brethren. This makes it a crucial and urgent mission for the Nigerian Church.

---

[345] Patterson, "Preaching as Nonviolent Resistance," 99.

The Power of Lament

Human experience reveals that life is not always fair to us. We can all tell when things get out of our control, when we are beset with troubles and cares, frustrations and pain. We have our tales of disorientation in life. For some, the unfair and unpleasant moments and experiences outweigh the joyous and pleasant life situations. We sometimes and in some circumstances mask our feelings and emotions from the people's awareness. It is however different when we appear before God. At prayer, it is hardly possible to pretend about our real life experiences of pain and suffering. Our unpleasant moments and memories become raw material for prayer.

Lament is a form of prayer by which we pour our hearts to God as raw as our conditions are. Lament is a protestation, which rests on God's power and willingness to intervene in human conditions. It has to do with the hope that God will hear and act on behalf of his people who call upon him.[346] Lament is a voice to human suffering and grief. An abused person who finds herself in a cycle of violence has more sorrowful tales and disorientation. Lament, thus becomes a poignant expression of her grief. Sharing one's story of abuse with neighbors who have internalized the dominant narrative of women's abuse by men will only beget advice and recommendations that would keep the sufferer perpetually docile and submissive to the

---

[346] John F. Craghan, *Psalms for All Seasons* (Collegeville, MN: Liturgical Press, 1993), 99.

abuse culture. It is usually advisable to seek the support of trained ministers and therapists.

In addition to seeking the assistance of caregivers and professionals, abused persons can help themselves both as individuals and as a group by tapping from the power of lament (even therapists recommend lament to their clients). Laments have tremendous healing power. In lament, we talk directly to God – the God who is with us – in our woundedness with the hope to salve our wounds. As God's adopted children, we have all the right to address God from the depths of our sorrow and grief and expect a soothing response from him. Certainly because he enjoins us to come to him with our troubles and cares for his support.[347] According to the Pslamist, God has a record of our laments and stores our tears in his wineskin.[348] What is more consoling is that God is united to us in our suffering. Our disorientation is God's disorientation. Nicholas Wolterstorff, a professor of Philosophical Theology, in the *Lament for a Son* (being his Lament for his twenty-five year-old Eric who died while climbing a mountain in Austria) writes thus: "We're in it together, God and we, together in the history of our world. The history of our world is the history of our suffering together. Every act of evil extracts a tear from God, every plunge into anguish extracts a sob from God."[349]

The ability to make a lament bespeaks the courage to break free from fear and disorientation. It demonstrates the capacity to break

---

[347] Ps 55:22

[348] Ps 56:9 (Community Christian Bible)

[349] Nicholas Wolterstorff, *Lament For a Son* (Grand Rapids, MI: William B. Eerdmans Publ. Comp, 1987), 91.

away from our old securities because they have failed us. A resort to lament shows that we are now able to see our suffering and pain as the starting point of our reorientation; it points to the confidence to lean on God, a dependence that implies a growth in our relationship rather than a loss of our human autonomy. Laments have transformative power, helping us move from disorientation to reorientation.

Scripture contains a significant number of laments especially in the Psalms for our use. Individuals and groups can pray the biblical laments as well compose their own laments that flow from their experience. In the Bible, laments have the following basic structure: address with an introductory cry for help, lament, confession of trust or assurance of being heard, petition, and a vow of praise.[350] Biblical laments include: Psalms 3, 22, 39, 42, 43, 69, 85, 88 and most passages of the book of Job among others. Some of the laments contain an expression of anger as the psalmist pours out his mind. This raises the question of whether anger has a place in the prayer life of the people of God. Querying the culture of bottling our emotions during suffering and griefing Wolterstorff asks the rhetoric question, 'Why insist on never outwarding the inward when the inward is bleeding?'[351] The following response from John Craghan is insightful as it draws from both theology and the social sciences:

---

[350] Craghan, *Psalms*, 100.

[351] Wolterstorff, *Lament*, 26.

Anger occupies a legitimate place in our prayer life. Too often we have been seduced into thinking that emotion opposes reason. According to Israel's traditions the emotion brought about by the Hebrews' lament (see Ex 2:6) moves the Lord to act on behalf of his people. According to sound psychology we must reply to life's threats through anger. Anger thereby becomes a significant component in our human growth. To suppress anger does not contribute to an integral human life. According to covenant theology God's people have the right to express their grief in a community setting. The destructive tendencies of social evil are thus articulated in a forum where sufferers can hope for the bottoming out of disorientation. Ultimately anger does not necessarily stifle the human spirit since it is capable of rendering us yet more human.[352]

In our disorientation and our search for justice, it is not illegitimate to express our anger against persons, institutions responsible for our suffering and pain or against God when he seems to be silence or absent. In lament, we seek the face of the seemingly absent God. At prayer, we seek for an assurance of the presence of our God. In his lament, Job expressed his frustration and disorientation; he sought for a sign of God's presence in the face of his affliction. Job expressed his anger over his confusion and darkness without offending his maker.[353] The experience of the Psalmist and of John of the

---

[352] Craghan, *Psalms*, 119.

[353] Job 2:10.

Cross reveal that ultimately, the absence of God is his presence un-recognized. God reveals his loving and comforting presence when we come to him broken and raw as we are trusting his power and love. Lament therefore is revealing and comforting.

Ultimately, lament challenges us to identify with those who suf-fer. Since the sufferer's problem becomes God's, 'we're in it to-gether,' to use Wolterstorff's expression, the other person's affliction becomes my affliction and their community's suffering becomes my community's. "To know the Lord in prayer is also to be aware of the Lord's extended family, with their needs."[354] The history of the world, says Wolterstorff, is the history of our deliverance together.[355] United as individuals, communities and as one human family, we must unite to lament against the suffering and pain inflicted on hu-mans by their fellows. Together we can end abuse and ensure the emancipation and empowerment of abused persons in our commu-nities and in our world.

---

[354] Craghan, *Psalms*, 100.

[355] Wolterstorff, *Lament*, 91.

APPENDIX I

Healing Rite for victims and survivors of domestic violence

Preparation for the rite (facilitator engages the suggested Scripture reading)

Genesis 34: *¹Dinah, who was Jacob's daughter by Leah, went out to visit some of the women of that region. ²Shechem, the son of Hamor the Hivite, headman of the region, saw her, seized her and forced her to sleep with him. ⁵Meanwhile, Jacob had heard how his daughter Dinah had been dishonored, but since his sons were out in the countryside with his livestock, Jacob said nothing until they came back. ⁷When Jacob's sons returned from the countryside and heard the news, the men were outraged and infuriated that Shechem had insulted Israel by sleeping with Jacob's daughter – a thing totally unacceptable.*

OR

2 Samuel 13: *⁷David then sent word to Tamar at the palace, 'Go to your brother Ammon's house and prepare some food for him. ⁸Tamar went to the house of her brother Ammon who was lying there in bed. She took dough and kneaded it, and she made some cakes while he watched, and baked the cakes. ¹⁰So Tamar took the cakes which she had made and brought them to her brother Ammon in the inner room. ¹¹And as she was offering the food to him, he caught hold of her and said, 'Come to bed with me, sister! ¹²She replied, 'No, brother! Do*

235

not force me! This is no way to behave in Israel. Do not do anything so disgraceful. ¹³ Wherever should I go? I should be marked with shame, while you would become disgrace in Israel. Why not go and speak to the king? He will not refuse to give me to you. ¹⁴ But he would not listen to her; he overpowered her and raped her. ¹⁹ Tamar put dust on her head, tore the magnificent dress which she was wearing, laid her hand on her head, and went away, crying aloud as she went.

Opening Song: Amazing Grace³⁵⁶

Amazing grace how sweet the sound,
That saved a wretch like me!
I once was lost, but now am found;
Was blind, but now I see.

'Twas grace that taught my heart to fear,
And grace my fears relieved;
How precious did that grace appear
The hour I first believed!

Through many dangers, toils and snares,
I have already come;
'Tis grace hath brought me safe thus far,
And grace will lead me home.

---

[356] Amazing Grace by John Newton (1779), is a common church song that most parishioners are conversant with.

The Lord has promised good to me,
His Word my hope secures;
He will my Shield and Portion be,
As long as life endures.

Yea, when this flesh and heart shall fail,
And mortal life shall cease,
I shall possess, within the veil,
A life of joy and peace.

The earth shall soon dissolve like snow,
The sun forbear to shine;
But God, Who called me here below,
Will be forever mine.

When we've been there ten thousand years,
Bright shining as the sun,
We've no less days to sing God's praise
Than when we'd first begun.

Opening Scriptur/ Prayer: The Beatitudes
Facilitator: Matthew 5:1-12 tells us that, "Seeing the crowds, he
[Jesus] went onto the mountain. And when he was seated his disciples came to him. [2] Then he began to speak. This is what he taught
them:
[3] " How blessed are the poor in spirit:
  the kingdom of heaven is theirs.

[4] Blessed are the gentle:

they shall have the earth as inheritance.

[5] Blessed are those who mourn:

they shall be comforted.

[6] Blessed are those who hunger and thirst for righteousness:

they shall have their fill.

[7] Blessed are the merciful:

they shall have mercy shown them.

[8] Blessed are the pure in heart:

they shall see God.

[9] Blessed are the peacemakers:

they shall be recognized as children of God.

[10] Blessed are those who are persecuted in the cause of uprightness:

the kingdom of heaven is theirs.

[11] "Blessed are you when people abuse you and persecute you and speak all kinds of calumny against you falsely on my account. [12] Rejoice and be glad, for your reward will be great in heaven; this is how they persecuted the prophets before you.

Facilitator: Let us not forget that Jesus spoke these words to a crowd.

Participants: We recognize that abuses are widespread, and we lament.

Facilitator: Let us pray together, asking God to bless those who are hurting among us, just as Jesus blessed those who were hurting in his context on the mountain. Lord, bless those whose spirits have been broken.

Participants: Bring your kingdom close to their hearts.

Facilitator: Lord, bless those on whose grief we cannot and will not put a limit.

Participants: Bring comfort by drawing close to them and using us to create the comforting community they need.

Facilitator: Lord, bless those who have been silenced and silent.

Participants: Let us create safe spaces for them to speak.

Facilitator: Lord, bless those stripped of their dignity and left feeling empty.

Participants: May we offer them life-giving words and actions to make them whole again.

Facilitator: Lord, bless those who will bravely share their suffering and pain.

Participants: Let us be attentive and merciful as we listen to and believe their stories.

Facilitator: Lord, bless the innocent ones harmed by no fault of theirs.

Participants: Bring justice to them, may they see you in a healing path moving forward from these traumatic events, and may they overcome the unjustified feelings of guilt and shame.

Facilitator: Lord, bless those whose peace has given way to anxiety.

Participants: May we usher in peace at this moment, and may they, in turn, offer the same hope and peace to others, in time.

Facilitator: Lord, bless all who suffer any form of domestic violence.

Participants: May they take solace in knowing that you are near and a companion.

All: Amen.

Invocation/Exhortation

Facilitator: Sisters, the Bible does not condone any form of abuse, be it verbal, sexual, physical or emotional. Furthermore, "The Bible neither covers up nor ignores sexual assault. In fact, biblical law shows how the Lord takes up the cause of the victim and the vulnerable. Deuteronomy 22:25-27 safeguarded the survivor of sexual assault from being unjustly blamed or ignored. In ancient Israel, this law established a pattern, an ethical framework by which God's people could discern specific situations that it didn't specifically address."[357] Let us listen to these scriptural passages and derive strength, healing, and hope.

(The facilitator invites participant(s) to read the following passages from Scripture.)

Isaiah 43:2-3a: Do not be afraid, for I have redeemed you; I have called you by your name, you are mine. Should you pass through the waters, I shall be with you; or through rivers, they will not swallow you up. Should you walk through fire, you will not suffer, and the flame will not burn you. For I am Yahweh, your God.

---

[357] Katie Maccoy, "God is not silent: what the Bible teaches about sexual assault," in The Ethics and Religious Liberty Commision, Dec 11, 2017. Retrieved from https://erlc.com/resource-library/articles/god-is-not-silent-what-the-bible-teaches-about-sexual-assault.

Psalm 82:3-4 "Let the weak and the orphan have justice, be fair to the wretched and the destitute. Rescue the weak and the needy; save them from the clutches of the wicked.

Prayer[358]

God of endless love,

ever caring, ever strong,

always present, always just:

You gave your only Son

to save us by the blood of his cross.

Gentle Jesus, shepherd of peace,

join to your own suffering

the pain of all who have been hurt

in body, mind, and spirit

by those who betrayed the trust placed in them.

Hear the cries of our brothers and sisters

who have been gravely harmed,

and the cries of those who love them.

Soothe their restless hearts with hope,

steady their shaken spirits with faith.

Grant them justice for their cause,

enlightened by your truth.

---

[358] Culled from "Prayer for Healing Victims Of Abuse," by the United States Conference of Catholic Bishops, http://www.usccb.org/prayer-and-worship/prayers-and-devotions/prayers/prayer-for-healing-victims-of-abuse.cfm.

Holy Spirit, comforter of hearts,
heal your people's wounds
and transform brokenness into wholeness.
Grant us the courage and wisdom,
humility and grace, to act with justice.
Breathe wisdom into our prayers and labors.
Grant that all harmed by abuse may find peace in justice.
We ask this through Christ, our Lord. Amen.

Allow time and space for any person/persons to share whatever part/parts of their story that they deem appropriate for expressing grief and the desire to heal. Invite them by name to share their narratives.

Facilitator: It takes courage to share your personal story of pain.

Supportive Participants: We hear you, and we believe you. We do not condone the suffering you (sharer's name) have endured. We recognize that your experience is unacceptable, and we will not explain it away, but we will gather ourselves to you in whatever way you need us, for the sake of your healing.

Prayer over focal person:
Eternal and merciful God, we come to you today as a community, as people who are connected intricately in relationship and who know what brokenness is—what it feels like, what it looks like, how it sounds. We have heard (Name)'s story and we mourn with her. We

know you are present with us and mourn with us. Our deep desire is to participate with you in bringing comfort and healing to (Name). This may not be easy, and we recognize that it is a process. Open our hearts to this sister of ours, and may we always be found when she is in need of our love. Powerfully and graciously, work in all of our lives so that (Name) will know that she is not alone and that her testimony has been heard and believed. As we pray for her, we lament her suffering, and we turn to you for healing and wholeness, for we believe that by acting together we can be a community that brings restoration and joy. Let it begin with us, and let it begin today with (Name). We ask this through Christ our Lord. Amen.

(Participants may join hands with the focal person as the say the above prayer)

Closing Psalm 124:1-8 (read together)

[1] If it had not been the LORD who was on our side—
     let Israel now say—
[2] if it had not been the LORD who was on our side
     when people rose up against us,
[3] then they would have swallowed us up alive,
     when their anger was kindled against us;
[4] then the flood would have swept us away,
     the torrent would have gone over us;
[5] then over us would have gone
     the raging waters.

[6] Blessed be the LORD,
> who has not given us
> as prey to their teeth!
[7] We have escaped like a bird
> from the snare of the fowlers;
the snare is broken,
> and we have escaped!
[8] Our help is in the name of the LORD,
> who made heaven and earth.

(At the end of the readings, the facilitator invites all present to ponder on the words that have been read.)

Prayer *(After pondering on the words that have been read, the leader gives a brief words of exhortation, and invites one of the participants to say the following prayer)*

"Dear Lord, there are times when this life is filled with joy, times of gladness and celebration. But there are other times, many other times, times of sadness and loss, times of mourning and weeping. Along with the whole creation, our hearts ache for the day when your kingdom will fully come. Then you will wipe away every tear. Sorrow and sadness will pass away. In our mourning, we thank you for the hope you give us through Christ. But we also thank you for the comfort you give us right now. Indeed, how grateful we are for the Comforter, the Spirit who dwells within us to grant us your peace.... All praise to you Lord, because you comfort those who mourn. Amen."[359]

All: Amen

Concluding Prayer/Blessing

Facilitator: *(Bow your heads and pray for God's blessing).* God is nearer to those who are of a broken heart and crushed spirit (Psalm 34:18). God heals the brokenhearted and binds up their wounds (Psalm 147:3). The Apostle Paul wrote that God "comforts us in all our affliction, so that we may be able to comfort those who are in any affliction, with the comfort with which we ourselves are comforted by God" (2 Cor. 1:4). Following the comfort Paul received from Philemon in his distress, Paul wrote, "For I have derived much joy and comfort from your love, my brother, because the hearts of the saints have been refreshed through you" (Phil 1:7). "God has amazing plans for you (Jeremiah 29:11) and the pain you feel now is not what God has in store for you."[360]

Facilitator: May your hearts be refreshed through the love and prayers of all who gathered for you today!

All: Amen.

---

[359] Mark D. Roberts, "Blessed Are Those Who Mourn," *The High Calling,* May 18, 2018, www.thologyofwor.org.

[360] Timothy Tomlinson, "Trauma Healing: Complete Healing for Your Mind, Body & Soul," Timothy Tomlinson Ministries, 2019, www.timothy-tomlinson.org.

Facilitator: May you who have walked out of darkness embrace the world with joy, peace and hope!

All: Amen.

Facilitator: May your voices be heard!

All: Amen.

Facilitator: May your stories be witnessed!

All: Amen.

Facilitator: May you be remembered!

All: Amen.

Facilitator: May the light of the Lord shine upon you!

All: Amen.

Facilitator: May you love and be loved forevermore!

All: Amen.

Closing Song: Lord of all Hopefulness[361]

Lord of all hopefulness, Lord of all joy,

Whose trust, ever childlike, no cares could destroy:

Be there at our waking, and give us, we pray,

Your bliss in our hearts, Lord, at the break of the day.

Lord of all eagerness, Lord of all faith,

Whose strong hands were skilled at the plane and the lathe,

Be there at our labors, and give us, we pray,

Your strength in our hearts, Lord, at the noon of the day.

---

[361] The song by Jan Struther (1901-53) is a hymn for night prayer in the breviary (The Liturgy of the Hours).

Lord of all kindliness, Lord of all grace,

Your hands swift to welcome, your arms to embrace,

Be there at our homing, and give us, we pray,

Your love in our hearts, Lord, at the eve of the day.

Lord of all gentleness, Lord of all calm,

Whose voice is contentment, whose presence is balm,

Be there at our sleeping, and give us, we pray,

Your peace in our hearts, Lord, at the end of the day.

It is understandable if the women group does not take all the above prayer/ritual in their particular prayer meeting due to constraint of time. They could start from where they ended at their previous meeting. We however encourage those who constitute a WSG to to take the entire prayer exercise each time they gather.

APPENDIX II

Recommended Hymns and Psalms

Be Not Afraid (Dufford)

Be Still My Soul [Finlandia]

Blest Are They (Haas)

Center of My Life (Inwood)

Christ Be Beside Me [Bunessan or St. Rose]

Christ Be Our Light (Farrell)

Christ In the Rubble [September Hope]

The Church of Christ in Every Age [Dunedin]

Come Down, O Love Divine [Down Ampney]

Come, My Way, My Truth, My Life [The Call]

Come to Me, O Weary Traveler (Dunstan/Moore)

Dona Nobis Pacem (Traditional)

Eye Has Not Seen (Haugen)

God Is Love [Abbot's Leigh]

Great God of Mercy [Christe Sanctorum]

Healer of Our Every Ill (Haugen)

Hold Me in Life (Huijbers)

Hold us in Your Mercy: Penitential Litany (Cooney)

How Can I Keep From Singing [Endless Song]

How Good the Name of Jesus Sounds [St. Peter]

I Am the Light of the World (Hayakawa)

I Heard the Voice of Jesus [Kingsfold]

In the Lord I'll Be Ever Thankful (Taizé)

Is This A Day of New Beginnings [Steeple Bells]

Jesus, Come To Us (Haas)

Jesus, Lead the Way [Rochelle]

Jesus, Remember Me (Taizé)

The King of Love, My Shepherd Is [St. Columba]

Lead Me, Guide Me (Akers)

The Living God My Shepherd Is [Brother James' Air]

Lord of All Hopefulness [Slane]

Nada Te Turbe (Taizé)

May the Lord, Mighty God [Wen-Ti]

My Shepherd Will Supply My Need [Resignation]

O Blessed Are the Poor in Spirit [Kontakion] (Byzantine/Slavonic Chant)

O Christ the Great Foundation [Aurelia]

O Christ, the Healer [Erhalt Uns Herr]

O Day of Peace that Dimly Shines [Jerusalem]

O God, Our Help In Ages Past [St. Anne]

O God, You Search Me (Farrell)

O Lord, Hear My Prayer (Taizé)

Our Darkness (Taizé)

Prayer of Saint Francis (Temple)

Psalm 42: As the Deer Longs [O Waly Waly]

Shelter Me, O God (Hurd)

There Is A Balm in Gilead [Balm in Gilead]

Ubi Caritas (Taizé)

Veni Creator Spiritus (Chant)

We Cannot Measure How You Heal (Bell)

You Are Near (Schutte)

Within Our Darkest Night (Taizé)

Words to Build a Life On (Mike Crawford and His Secret Siblings)

Psalms:

Psalm 16 – Lord, you will show us the path of life.

Psalm 16 – You are my inheritance, O Lord.

Psalm 17 – Lord, when your glory appears, my joy will be full.

Psalm 18 – I love you, Lord, my strength.

Psalm 23 – The Lord is my shepherd, there is nothing I shall want.

 OR: Though I walk in the valley of darkness, I fear no evil, for you are with me.

Psalm 25 – To you, O Lord, I lift my soul.

Psalm 27 – The Lord is my light and my salvation.

Psalm 33 – Lord, let your mercy be on us, as we place our trust in you.

Psalm 34 – The Lord hears the cry of the poor.

Psalm 63 – My soul is thirsting for you, O Lord.

Psalm 80 – Lord, make us turn to you; let us see your face and we shall be saved.

Psalm 85 – Lord, let us see your kindness, and grant us your salvation.

Psalm 91 – Be with me, Lord, when I am in trouble.

Psalm 103   The Lord is kind and merciful.

Psalm 116 – I will walk before the Lord, in the land of the living.

Psalm 131 – In you, O Lord, I have found my peace.

Psalm 146 – Lord, come and save us.

BIBLIOGRAPHY

Adam, Klaus-Peter. "The Earth and the Earthling: Thoughts on Gen 2-3." *Currents in Theology and Mission* 47, no. 1 (January 2020): 35-37.

Agbalajobi, Damilola, and Leke Oluwalogbon. "The Nigerian Senate and the Politics of the Non-passage of the Gender Equality Bill." *African Journal of Political Science and International Relations* 13, no. 3 (April 2019): 17-23. https://www.academicjournals.org/AJPSIR.

Aihie, Ose N. "Prevalence of Domestic Violence in Nigeria: Implications for Counselling." *Edo Journal of Counselling* 2, no. 1 (May 2009): 86-93. https://jstor.org/stable/41321371.

Akinade, Emmanuel, Temitayo Adewuyi, and Afolashade Sulaiman. "Social-Legal Factors that Influence the Perpetuation of Rape in Nigeria." *Science Direct* 5, (March 2010): 1760-1764. www.sciencedirect.com.

Arbuckle, Gerald. *Culture, Inculturation, and Theologians: A Postmodern Critique.* Collegeville, PA: Liturgical Press, 2010.

Archer, Margret. *Being Human: The Problem of Agency.* Cambridge, UK: Cambridge University Press, 2000.

Bancroft, Lundy. *When Dad Hurts Mom: Helping Your Children Heal the Wounds of Witnessing Abuse.* New York: Putnam, 2004.

Behnke, Andrew, Natalie Ames, and Tina Hancock. "What Would They Do? Latino Church Leaders and Domestic Violence." *Journal of Interpersonal Violence* 27, no. 7 (2012): 1259-1275.

Bent-Goodley, Tracia, Noelle St. Vil, and Paulette Hubbert. "A Spirit Broken: The Black Church's Evolving Response to Domestic Violence." *Social Work and Christianity* 39, no. 1 (2012): 52-65.

Burns, J. Patout. "Theological Anthropology." In *T&T Clark Reader in Theological Anthropology*, edited by Marc Cortez and Michael Jensen, 25-32. New York: Bloomsbury T&T Clark, 2018.

Carrette, Jeremy. *Foucault and Religion: Spiritual Corporality and Political Spirituality*. New York: Routledge, 2000.

Cartwright, Sophie. "Soul and Body in Early Christianity: An Old and New Conundrum." In *A History of Mind and Body in Late Antiquity*, edited by Anna Marmodoro and Sophie Cartwright, 173-190. Cambridge, UK: Cambridge Press, 2018.

Castelli, Elizabeth. *Imitating Paul: A Discourse of Power*. Louisville, KY: John Knox Press, 1991.

Clinebell, Howard. *Basic Types of Pastoral Care and Counseling: Resources for the Ministry of Healing and Growth*. 3rd ed. Nashville, TN: Abingdon Press, 2011.

Cooper-White, Pamela. *The Cry of Tamar: Violence against Women and the Church's Response*. Minneapolis, MN: Fortress Press, 2012.

Cortez, Marc, and Michael Jensen. "Human Ontology." In *T&T Clark Reader in Theological Anthropology*, edited by Marc Cortez and Michael Jensen, 129-198. New York: Bloomsbury T&T Clark, 2018.

Craghan, F. John. *Psalms for All Seasons*. Collegeville, MN: Liturgical Press, 1993.

Cranton, Patricia. *Understanding and Promoting Transformative Learning: A Guide to Theory and Practice.* Sterling, VA: Stylus Publishing, 2016.

Danaher, Geoff, Tony Schirato and Jen Webb. *Understanding Foucault.* Thousand Oaks, CA: Sage Publications Ltd, 2000.

Dewey, John. *Experience and Education.* New York: Touchstone, 1997.

Dunlap, Susan. *Caring Cultures: How Congregations Respond to the Sick.* Waco, TX: Baylor University Press, 2009.

Eisner, Elliott. *The Educational Imagination: On the Design and Evolution of School Programs.* 2nd ed. New York: Macmillan Publishing Co, 1985.

Elliot, Mark. "The Character of the Biblical God." In *The Identity of Israel's God in Christian Scripture*, edited by Don Collett, Mark Elliot, Mark Gignilliat, and Ephraim Radner, 47-64. Atlanta: The Society of Biblical Literature, 2020.

Fortune, Marie. "The Importance of Religion and Faith." In *Walking Together: Working with Women from Diverse Religious and Spiritual Traditions, A Guide for Domestic Violence Advocates*, edited by Jean Anton. Seattle, WA: Faith Trust Institute, 2005.

Fowler, N. Dawnovise, and Michele A. Rountree. "Exploring the Meaning and Role of Spirituality for Women Survivors of Intimate Partner Abuse." In *The Journal of Pastoral Care and Counseling* 63, no. 3 (September 2009). https://doi.org/10.1177/15423050090630030.

Freire, Paulo. *Pedagogy of the Oppressed.* New York: Bloomsbury, 2012.

Furey, M. ConstanceBrian, Matz, Steven L. McKenzie, Thomas Romer, Jens Schroter, Barry Dov Walfish, and Eric Ziolkowski, eds. *Encyclopedia of the Bible and Its Reception.* vol. 18. Boston, MA: De Gruyter, 2020.

Green, Erin, Alisha Gaines, Tisa Hill, and Jaime Dollahite. "Personal, Proxy, and Collective Food Agency among Early Adolescents." *Appetite* 166 (January 2021): 1-10. https://doi.org/10.1016/j.appet.2021.105435.

Griffith, Colleen. "The Spirit and the Nearness of God." In *The Holy Spirit: Setting the World on Fire*, edited by Richard Lennan and Nancy Pineda-Madrid, 3-12. Mahwah, NJ: Paulist Press, 2017.

Groome, Thomas. *Christian Religious Education: Sharing Our Story and Vision.* San Francisco: Jossey-Bass Publishers, 1999.

------ *Sharing Faith: A Comprehensive Approach to Religious Education and Pastoral Ministry.* Eugene, OR: Wipf and Stock Publishers, 1998.

------ *Will There Be Faith? A New Vision for Educating and Growing Disciples.* New York: HarperCollins Publishers, 2011.

Guevin, Benedict. *Christian Anthropology and Sexual Ethics.* Lanham, MD: University of America Press, 2002.

Harrington, Daniel. *The Gospel of Matthew.* Sacra Pagina Series, vol. 1. Collegeville, PA: The Liturgical Press, 1991.

Hicks, Donna. *Dignity: Its Essential Role in Resolving Conflict.* New Haven, CT: Yale University Press, 2011.

Hille, Haker. "Compassion for Justice." In *Mercy.* Concilium Series, edited by Lisa Cahill, Diego Irarrazaval, and Joao Cha, 54-64. London: SCM Press, 2017.

Hooker, David. *The Little Book of Transformative Community Conferencing: A Hopeful, Practical Approach to Dialogue.* New York: Good Books, 2016.

Houston, Walter. *Contending for Justice: Ideologies and Theologies of Social Justice in the Old Testament.* New York: T&T Clark, 2006.

John Paul II. *Christifidelis Laici, Post-Synodal Exhortation.* Rome: Vatican Press, 1988.

------ *Familiaris Consortio, Post-Synodal Apostolic Exhortation.* Rome: Vatican Press, 1981.

------ *Mulieris Dignitatem, Apostolic Letter. Rome:* Vatican Press, 1988.

Johnson, Timothy Luke. *The Revelatory Body: Theology as Inductive Art.* Cambridge, UK: William B. Eerdmans Publishing Co, 2015.

Joseph, Simon. *The Nonviolent Messiah: Jesus, Q, and the Enochic Tradition.* Minneapolis, MN: Fortress Press, 2014.

Kennedy, James, Robert Davis, and Bruce Taylor. "Changes in Spirituality and Well-Being among Victims of Assault." *Journal for the Scientific Study of Religion* 37, no. 2 (June 1998). https://www.jstor.org/stable/1387531.

Kimball, Charles. *When Religion Becomes Evil.* San Francisco: HarperSanFrancisco, 2002.

Klawans, Jonathan. "Moral and Ritual Purity." In *The Historical Jesus in Context,* edited by Amy-Jill Levine, Dale Allison, and John Crossan, 266-284. Princeton, NJ: Princeton University Press, 2006.

Kroeger, Catherine, and Nancy Nagon-Clark. *No Place for Abuse.* Downers Grove, IL: Inter Varsity, 2010.

Layzell, Ruth. "Pastoral Counselling with Those Who have Experienced Abuse in Religious Settings." In *Clinical Counselling in Pastoral Settings,* edited by Gordon Lynch, 107-123. New York: Routledge, 1999.

Lee, Boyung. *Transforming Congregations through Community: Faith Formation from the Seminary to the Church.* Louisville, KY: John Knox Press, 2013.

Lehner-Hartmann, Andrea. "Familiar Violence against Women as a Challenge for Theology and Ethics." In *When 'Love' Strikes: Social Sciences, Ethics and Theology on Family Violence,* edited by Annemie Dillen, 109-130. Leuven, Belgium: Peeters, 2009.

Long, Thomas, and Thomas Lynch. *The Good Funeral: Death, Grief, and the Community of Care.* Louisville, KY: John Knox Press, 2013.

Longchar, Wati. "Unclean and Compassionate Hand of God." *The Ecumenical Review* 63, no. 4 (December 2011): 408-418.

Marthaler, L. Bernard, Gregory F. LaNave, Jonathan Y. Tan, Richard E. McCarron, and Denis J. Obermeyer, eds. *The New Catholic Encyclopedia.* 2nd ed. vols. 8 and 9. Detroit, MI: Gale, 2003.

Marshal, D. Amy, Jillian Panuzio, and Casey T. Taft. "Intimate Partner Violence among Military Veterans and Active Duty Servicemen." *Clinical Psychology Review* 25 (May 2005): 862-76.

McClure, John, and Nancy Ramsay, eds. *Telling the Truth: Preaching about Sexual and Domestic Violence.* Cleveland, OH: United Church Press, 1998.

McDonald, Joseph. "What is Moral Injury? Current Definitions, Perspectives and Context." *Moral Injury: A Guidebook for Understanding and Engagement*, edited by Brad Kelle, 7-20. Lanham, MD: Lexington books, 2020.

Meier, John. *A Marginal Jew: Rethinking the Historical Jesus*. vol. 3. New York: Doubleday, 2001.

------ *A Marginal Jew: Rethinking the Historical Jesus*. vol. 4. New Haven, CT: Yale University Press, 2009.

Nmadu, Grace Awawu, Abubakar Jafaru, Tukur Dahiru, Istifanus Anekoson Joshua, Amina Mohammed-Durosinlorun. "Cross-sectional Study on Knowledge, Attitude and Prevalence of Domestic Violence among Women in Kaduna, North-west Nigeria." *BMJ Open* (March 2022): 1-11.

Nouwen, Henri, Donald McNeil, and Douglas Morrison. *Compassion: A Reflection on the Christian Life*. New York: Doubleday, 1989.

Nussbaum, Martha. *Political Emotions: Why Love Matters for Justice*. Cambridge, MA: The Belknap of Harvard University Press, 2013.

Nwabichie, Remigius. *A Philosophy for the Christian Education of the Igbo of the Southeastern Nigeria: Thomas Groome's Shared Praxis Approach*. PhD diss, Fordham University, 2018.

Nwabunike, Collins, and Eric Tenkorang. "Domestic and Marital Violence among Three Ethnic Groups in Nigeria." *Journal of Interpersonal Violence* 32, no. 18 (2017): 2751-2776.

Oduyoye, Mercy Amba. *Daughters of Anowa: African Women and Patriachy*. Maryknoll, NY: Orbis Books, 1995.

Ojigho, Osai. "Prohibiting Domestic Violence through Legislation in Nigeria." *Agenda* no. 82 (2009):86-93.

Okemgbo, N. Christian, Adekunbi K. Omideyi, and Clifford O. Odimegwu. "Prevalence, Patterns and Correlates of Domestic Violence in Selected Igbo Communities in Imo State, Nigeria." *African Journal of Reproductive Health* 6, no. 2 (August 2002): 101-114.

Okome, Mojubaolu Olufunke. "Unknown Solidier: Women's Radicalism, Activism, and State Violence in Twentieth-Century Nigeria." In *Gender and Power Relations in Nigeria*, edited by Ronke Iyabowale Ako-Nai, 239-266. Lanham, MD: Lexington books, 2013.

Oluremi, Fareo. "Domestic Violence against Women in Nigeria." *European Journal of Psychological Research* 2, no. 1 (2015): 24-33. www.idpublications.org.

Opara, Henry, ed. *Pastoral Care for Women: In the Light of "Dignity & Vocation of Women" (Mulieris Dignitatem) of John Paul II.* Lagos, Nigeria: Marco Concepts, 2021.

Osmer, Richard. *Practical Theology: An Introduction.* Grand Rapids, MI: Wm. B. Eerdmans Publishing Co., 2008.

Panata, Sara. "It Is Not Breasts or Vaginas that Women Use to Wash Dishes: Gender, Class, and Neocolonialism through the Women in Nigeria Movement (1982-1992)." *Journal of International Women's Studies* 23, no. 2 (February 2022): 87-102.

Paulsell, Stephanie. *Honoring the Body: Meditations on a Christian Practice.* San Francisco: Jossey-Bass, 2002.

Percy, Anthony. *Theology of the Body Made Simple: An Introduction to John Paul's 'Gospel of the Body.'* Leominster, UK: Gracewing Publishing, 2005.

Pope Francis. *Evangelii Gaudium, Apostolic Exhortation.* Vatican City: Libreria Editrice Vaticana, 2013.

------ *Walking with Jesus: A Way Forward for the Church.* Chicago: Loyola Press, 2015.

Quispe, Sofia. "The Connection with the Mercy and Compassion That Inhabits Us." In *Mercy.* Concilium Series, edited by Lisa Cahill, Diego Irarrazaval, and Joao Cha, 11-20. London: SCM Press, 2017.

Regan, Jane. "The Aim of Catechesis: Educating For an Adult Church." In *Horizons and Hopes: The Future of Religious Education*, edited by Thomas Groome and Harold Horell, 31-50. New York: Paulist Press, 2003.

Second Vatican Council. "Decree on the Church's Missionary Activity, *Ad Gentes Divinitus*, 7 December, 1965." In *Vatican Council II: The Conciliar and Postconciliar Documents*, edited by Austin Flannery, 813-862. New York: Costello Publishing Company, 1975.

------"Decree on the Ministry and Life of Priests, *Presbyterorum Ordinis*, 7 December, 1965." In *Vatican Council II: The Conciliar and Postconciliar Documents*, edited by Austin Flannery, 863-902. New York: Costello Publishing Company, 1975.

------ "Pastoral Constitution on the Church in the Modern World, *Gaudium et Spes*, 7 December, 1965." In *Vatican Council II: The*

Conciliar and Postconciliar Documents, edited by Austin Flannery, 903-1014. New York: Costello Publishing Company, 1975.

Senior, Donald, and Carroll Stuhlmueller. *The Biblical Foundations for Mission.* New York: Orbis Books, 1983.

Shakespeare, William. *Romeo and Juliet.* act 3, scene 5.

Sigel, Charles, and Mitchell Mackinem. *Did He Say That? The Difficult Words of Jesus.* Eugene, OR: Wipf & Stock, 2016.

Simpson, Nicole. "Life After Sexual Trauma and Incarceration: A Restorative Model For Wholeness For Women Who Suffered Sexual Violence." DMin Thesis, Boston University, 2020.

Sousa, Cindy, Todd Herrenkohl, Carrie Moylan, Emiko Tajima, Bart Klika, Roy Herrenkohl , and Jean Russo. "Longitudinal Study on the Effects of Child Abuse and Children's Exposure to Domestic Violence, Parent-Child Attachments, and Antisocial Behavior in Adolescence." *Journal of Interpersonal Violence* 26, no.1 (2011): 111-136. https://www.sagepub.com/journalspermissions.nav/doi.org/10.1177/0886260510362883.

Starkey, Denise. "The Roman Catholic Church and Violence against Women." In *Religion and Men's Violence against Women*, edited by Andy Johnson, 177-193. New York: Springer, 2016.

Sule, Balaraba, and Priscilla Starratt. "Islamic Leadership Positions for Women in Contemporary Kano State." In *Hausa Women in the Twentieth Century*, edited by Catherine Coles and Beverly Mack, 29-49. Madison: The University of Wisconsin Press, 1991.

Summit, Roland. "The Child Sexual Abuse Accommodation Syndrome." *Attachment: New Directions in Psychology and Relational Psychoanalysis* 7, no. 2 (July 2013): 125-147.

Tillman, Jane. "Intergenerational Transmission of Suicide: Moral Injury and the Mysterious Object in the Work of Walker Percy." *Journal of the American Psychoanalytic Association* 64, no. 3 (June 2016): 541-567.

Timmers-Huigens, Dorothea. "Christian Faith and Justification of Domestic Violence." In *When Love Strikes: Social Sciences, Ethics and Theology on Family Violence*, edited by Annemie Dillen, 169-193. Leuven, Belgium: Peeters, 2009.

Tran, Mai-Anh Le. *Reset the Heart: Unlearning Violence, Relearning Hope.* Nasville, TN: Abingdon, 2017.

Ukwuije, Bede. "Theofiliance and the Reconfiliation Dynamic: Healing Humanity's Divisions through the Memory of the Cross." In *Emerging Conversations on Theofiliation: Essays in Honour of Archbishop Anthony J.V. Obinna*, edited by Kenneth Ameke and Samuel Uzoukwu, 223-245. Bloomington, IN: Xlibris, 2019.

United States Conference of Catholic Bishops. *When I Call for Help: A Pastoral Response to Domestic Violence against Women.* Washington, D.C., 2002.

Vaughan, Olufemi. *Religion and the Making of Nigeria.* Durham, NC: Duke University Press, 2016.

Walton, Jonathan. *A Lens of Love: Reading the Bible in Its World for Our World.* Louisville, KY: John Knox Press, 2018.

Washington, Michael. "Care with Persons both Healthy and Unhealthy." *Covenant Quarterly* 76, nos. 3-4 (August-November 2018). http://www.covquarterly.com.

West, Traci. "Sustaining an Ethic of Resistance against Domestic Violence in Black Faith-Based Communities." In *Domestic Violence at the Margins*, edited by Natalie Sokoloff, 340-349. New Brunswick, NJ: Rutgers University Press, 2005.

Wimberly, Anne. *Soul Stories: African American Christian Education*. Nashville, TN: Abingdon Press, 1994.

Wolterstorff, Nicholas. *Lament for a Son*. Grand Rapids, MI: William B. Eerdmans Publ. Comp, 1987.

Wood, Susan. "The Priestly Identity: Sacrament of Ecclesial Community." *Worship* 69, no. 2 (March 1995): 109-127. https://digital.journalworship.org.

Wright, N.T. *Jesus and the Victory of God*. Minneapolis, MN: Fortress Press, 1996.

ABOUT THE AUTHOR

Henry Onwusoro Ogbuji is a priest of the Catholic Archdiocese of Owerri, Nigeria. Ordained in 2003, he has served his diocese in various pastoral and administrative capacities as associate pastor, pastor and associate Diocesan Finance Administrator. One of the major pastoral challenges he has had as a pastor involved ministering to victims of domestic violence. Hence, it became an area of interest for him during his graduate studies in the US. He obtained a Master's degree in Theology at Boston College (2017) and a doctorate in Transformational Leadership from Boston University (2022). Upon graduation from Boston University, the author returned to his home diocese in Nigeria and has since been engaged in pastoral ministry. Writing is poignant aperture to share his uniquely striking ministerial and academic experiences with a wider audience.

Made in the USA
Middletown, DE
11 May 2023

30458826R00159